The Fuzzy Leg Experiment

How I Grew to Love Myself in Two Years

Elizabeth Crooks

For Lee

Thank you for believing in me,
even when I couldn't see it myself.
Thank you for loving me, when I didn't know how.
Thank you for showing me how beautiful I am,
in every moment.
We shared quite a ride, but it isn't over yet!
I Love You, Always

Table of Contents

The universe works in mysterious, funny ways sometimes.
As I finished writing this book I discovered this little gem:

"Your time is limited, so don't waste it living someone else's life. Don't be trapped by dogma – which is living with the results of other people's thinking. Don't let the noise of others' opinions drown out your inner voice. And most important, have the courage to follow your heart and intuition. They somehow already know what you truly want to become. Everything else is secondary."

- Steve Jobs

Preface

A Little Bit about Me:

I'm not petite. Quite the opposite really. I've been overweight since the fifth grade. I topped the scales at 242 pounds my sophomore year of college after the freshman 25. Then I lost 30 pounds in three months by not eating and over-exercising my body because I really hated myself.

I quickly realized that this wasn't working though. When your co-workers and friends start to mention how pale you look and you often get asked the question, "are you okay?" something is just a bit off.

Also at the age of ten (i.e. fifth grade), my breasts started developing and one was not quite growing like the other. My mother blamed the hormones in chicken she ate while she was pregnant with me.

Whatever the reason, my left breast was left behind in a sense over the years. These days it would be considered a "B" cup, while my right breast is more of a "C" cup. I think they are vastly different but most women have two different sized breasts…or so

I've heard.

It is comforting on one level and then on the other hand I don't really believe it, because my mind believes I am an un-loveable freak. But hey, we all have something we need to work on in our lives. And while I may be okay with fuzzy legs now, after two years of conscious awareness and practice, I am still not okay with my breast size(s). But that is my opportunity for growth as I continue to learn new ways to love myself more.

No matter what you are going through, everyone has something they think is the worst thing in the world in regards to their own bodies. We all have our demons, our shadows, and the little voice in our head that comes up with reasons on how we're not good enough. Those reasons are lies, by the way.

The truth is that we are all worthy of love, and we can start by loving ourselves first. We may understand that everyone is battling their own minds in some way, and that we should be kind to them for this. But we often forget to be kind to ourselves.

We tell other people they are beautiful and wish they could see it themselves, and then go home and groan at our own appearance in the bathroom mirror. We encourage others while simultaneously putting ourselves down, often unconsciously.

If there is one thing I learned in two years, is that we are just as important as we make others to be. I may have things to work on physically, but I am in no way any less worthy of love and respect.

And that is where this book comes in.

The Experiment:

I started this experiment in April 2014 because I wanted to figure out why I cared so much about what other people thought of me. A lot of things came together at this time which ultimately added to the formation of this experiment.

My body developed a rash to the natural crystal deodorant I was using for the past few years prior to this experiment. I had slowly become a vegetarian and mostly vegan since 2009 and got on a kick about all-natural products and non-GMOs and yet I still gained weight and developed unhealthy habits. Just because food is vegan or all-natural, doesn't mean that it is good for every-body.

Anyway, I decided to just go back to basics. Minimal basics, that is. I did use coconut oil on my skin and underarms after a few months of going without anything. I also stopped wearing makeup and stopped using a hair dryer. Sure, I brushed my hair but I just let it do its thing after that. No products, just me.

Now, I believe I started shaving my legs when I was seven or eight. I saw it everywhere… magazines, television, school, and even my own mother. I found disposable razors in my parent's bathroom cabinet and it just went from there. I wasn't very good at it. I nicked myself often, but then you see the advertisements for cream to prevent nicks and scratches so you just think it happens to everybody... like this is somehow normal and what you were supposed to do.

And the more you shave, the more you often continue shaving. Bright white legs and dark brown hair are such a contrast that it was really difficult to watch my hair grow and stay that way for so long. It is amazing how many people expect to see a grown woman with smooth legs that wearing shorts with fuzz is looked upon often in disgust. But then again, that is their problem, not mine. We'll get to that.

I stopped wearing a bra at this time as well because I read a study where it was better for your breast health to do so. This article described how wearing bras were not good for your health because they restricted flow through the lymph nodes and actually decreased the elasticity and support of the breasts by preventing natural muscle formation. In other words, going without a bra prevents sagging breasts later in life compared to wearing a bra because the breasts are allowed to develop their strength from gravity and the natural flow of movement.

With having such a major issue with my breasts in general, in particular their differences in size, going without a bra was not something I had ever planned on. So while I stopped shaving my legs for two years, I also didn't wear a bra throughout this entire time. Occasionally I gave into camisoles when going out during the summer or out to dinner with a nice blouse over, but ultimately I tried to stop doing that as well. I needed to get okay with my breasts just being out there. And yeah, I got some looks, both positive and negative, along the way.

All in all I wanted an au natural approach to my life. I didn't know what to expect at the time I began this experiment. I had hoped to get over my issues quickly so I could go back to how things were. Oh how naïve I was!

I've learned so much these past two years, and the truth is there is no going back after you've grown in ways you didn't think were possible. I invite you to join me on this crazy ride as I recount my experiences and wisdom over the years as the hair on my legs grew, my breasts freely moved whichever way they pleased, and I discovered what it really means to be comfortable and love yourself just as you are, naturally.

Sweatpants Guru:

So, why did I wear sweatpants all the time, everywhere I went for this experiment? Because it was in my programming from a child that people don't wear sweatpants out in public, as if I would be looked down upon by doing so. I came from a middle-class family. My parents tried to give me all the things they never had growing up.

And while, materially, I was better off than they were, they still reiterated the beliefs, stories, and expectations their parents had for them: what it means to be successful, how to present yourself in public, what defines your worthiness and so on and so forth.

I love my parents completely. They taught me many things and loved me in their own way. But as an adult, I had to learn to unravel everything they taught me, sort through all my beliefs and their beliefs, in order to find out what was true for me from the very core of my being.

And this is where the sweatpants came in. I was always concerned with how I looked. I covered up my body at the same time because I didn't like the way I looked and I wanted as little attention as possible. Jeans, t-shirts, and sneakers were my main wardrobe.

My hair was always in a ponytail throughout school and college, and every day at work and even on dates. My hair was down for prom and school pictures but that was a result of pressure from outside forces. I was comfortable with the ponytail and bland clothes. I wanted easy and subtle.

Now, I had a couple pairs of sweatpants that just sat in my closet for years. And while I had them, and I always wanted to wear, I could never bring myself to do so because, even lounging around the house with my family or boyfriend at the time, I wanted to keep up appearances in jeans. Honestly it sounds a lot crazier in my mind.

I had a belief that wearing sweatpants made me less of a person: less worthy, less beautiful, less respectful… pretty much less of everything. I was envious of other people who could just wear their pajamas to the grocery store or strut down the street rocking cute sweatpants and not give a shit. I just couldn't do it. But I wanted to. And so I added this to the list of things to do during this overall experiment.

I had to flip the script, the literal script of my life, upside-down and inside-out in order to figure out why I did the things I did, and why I cared so much about what other people thought of me. We all do things, or not do things, out of fear of perceived rejection or judgment. I am now a big proponent of doing the things you are afraid of (within reason and your comfort zone) in order to overcome your fears.

If I couldn't get comfortable walking around in loose sweatpants, then what would it take for me to be comfortable in general? Certainly not walking around public naked…first of all that is kind of illegal, or at least severely frowned upon by society.

If you can't get comfortable in your own skin without clothes, then start with clothing that makes you uncomfortable. Some manner of clothing is present at our base comfort level and we just have to work backwards towards nakedness.

Everyone has their own comfort line and sweatpants crossed that line in my mind. Even wearing shorts in the Phoenix, Arizona summer time with exposed fuzzy legs pushed a lot of personal buttons and brought up a lot of stuff for me to deal with.

How This Book is Set Up:

While the wisdom I have learned is in a chronological fashion in this book, from when I started this experiment, I only make a reference to time on a few occasions. After all, knowledge is ultimately timeless. And although it may seem jumbled at first, everything comes together in the end.

Life is a jigsaw and we get pieces of the puzzle here and there throughout our lives. I share what I've learned as it has happened. You'll be surprised at your own epiphanies while reading this book in this fashion.

Don't let the two-years scare you away. While I needed two years of this "experiment" to get comfortable with my own body, you get the benefit of reading about two-years-worth of experiences, insight, and understandings in a short amount of time.

I know my journey is unique, just as yours is unique. I share what I have been through, what I feel I know, in hopes that it will assist you in your own way. I would also like to say that you don't have to do what I did to achieve the same kind of realization about yourself. I had to go to the extreme (for me) in order to get to that place where I can better love and accept myself as I am.

I needed to stop shaving, to stop wearing a bra, to wear sweatpants everywhere I went, to shower twice a week (if that sometimes), and so on and so forth to get to that place of self-love. I needed to know what it felt like physically, emotionally, and mentally what not taking care of myself meant in order to realize what I truly needed and not simply what I wanted out of life in regards to my body and what I thought it should be.

This was a journey of caring and not caring about myself simultaneously. I had a loving partner for six years prior to this experiment, and I knew he loved me because he told me so every change he got and showed it in more ways than I can remember. But he was shouting into the void. All the love in the world from this man, and all the love from others around me, didn't matter because I couldn't see it for myself.

I was lost in my own sea of unworthiness and unhappiness about my physical appearance and what I thought other people thought about me. I realized that all the love in the world from others wouldn't matter if I didn't learn to love myself first.

We all have our own struggles. Mine has certainly been physical appearance. I never thought I was good enough, attractive enough, or worthy enough for love. Not wearing a bra has been hard for me to do. Not shaving my legs has been hard for me. And I had to get okay with those kinds of things. I had to strip down to the basics, with minimal maintenance, to find out who I truly was and to get over the outward stuff that doesn't truly matter in the end.

So why share my experience? Sharing is scary, and yet it is freeing. Why would I share my intimate details with the world? Why would I expose thoughts about my personal story to strangers? To overcome my fears, that's why.

My journey over the years has been about finding out what I am and being comfortable with it, past all the fear, the doubt, and the lies we tell ourselves to get through the day. There is no need to care what other people think about you. Everyone is going through the same thing, in their own way.

And don't accept this as the end all, be all. Don't take anything as the ultimate truth. We each have to find our own truth, come to our own conclusions. These words I write helped me on my own path and I wish to share them with you. Please do not substitute the information within this book for professional advice, medical or otherwise.

Introduction

The experiment started in April 2014. I had already been experimenting off and on with not shaving my legs for long periods of time in the years before that. However, I usually wore jeans or long black pants if I was at work so no one else had to see them.

And, as you'll see in the introduction, it wasn't just my fuzzy legs that were part of the two-year-long trial to overcome my body issues. I believe we all have something we're ashamed about regarding our human bodies. I believe we are all ingrained from an early childhood to believe a certain way about ourselves, which results in many people not being happy with who they are and unable to accept their bodies as perfection, no matter what they look like or how they function.

In two years, I have come to realize and understand that the body is just a shell, or a vessel, that allows us to experience life on Earth. Every experience is unique. Every vessel is unique.

But still, even after "knowing" the body is just a shell logically, why did I still care what people think about me? Why was I so concerned about how I look in a stranger's eyes, someone who I may pass only once in a lifetime? Why did that matter to me?

Because I was taught to care what other people thought. I was taught to put others first. Maybe not intentionally, but it happened nonetheless.

Why did I feel so ashamed of my appearance? What is it about the body that is so thought-consuming that ultimately we can lose ourselves in it? Because we have been conditioned to hold our bodies to a particular standard.

We are all in silent agreement on what makes a person attractive or not attractive. We each have our own definitions based on our upbringings and beliefs. Why is no hair better than a lot of hair? And only on certain parts of the human body too.

I mean, summer was coming up, why would I stop shaving my legs before short-season? I felt the pressure to start shaving my legs almost immediately and all the fear boiled to the surface having to actually face fuzzy legs in the heat of the day. So why did I do this? Because I felt I had to in order to overcome my own issues. I had to go to the extremes in order to figure out the middle way for me on my own journey, just as we each have to find our own way.

Delving into Fear:

So, how do you not care what people think about you? You delve right into that pool of deep-seated fear that is within your own body, mind, and soul and you swim through it. You get your hands dirty. You sort through the muck and find the light at the end of the tunnel to the glittering clear ocean on the other side of that watery rabbit hole, where the mermaids swim and the sun never burns your skin, even if you stay outside all day with nothing on.

It is that amazing on the other side of fear, especially the fear of judgment. All fear boils down to the fear of judgment. Fear of rejection is just judgment of self-worth. Fear of failure is judgment of our abilities. Fear of pain is a judgment of experience. Fear of the unknown is the worst of all, because we've pre-judged everything that is unknown as scary, painful, and bad; all judgments without reason.

So this is why I did this experiment…I wanted to have less fear in my life. I needed to find what worked for me and I had to break everything back down to basics and sort it all out piece by piece.

Just one month prior to this experiment I got my first ever tattoo. I was 27.5 years old at the time and I had wanted a tattoo since I was 18 (at least…probably years before that but when you can legally get one it you really start seriously considering it). I always imagined a dragon on my back but it just never happened. Then, over nine years later, I realized that I was ready for a tattoo, and I also realized that getting one on my back was not what I desired anymore.

I wanted to see my tattoo every day. So I ended up getting a black and white cat with the word 'LOVE' on my right forearm. Now, to say I got over a lot of fear by doing this would be an understatement. I went through a series of thoughts and struggled with overcoming certain beliefs by doing this.

What would people think of me with a clearly visible tattoo on my arm? How differently would they see me now? I wouldn't be able to get certain jobs anymore, that was for sure. Or I would have to cover up my tattoo for others. Why did I care?

My family certainly freaked out after I posted the before and after photos of my bare-arm and tattooed-arm. And now, years later, people still look at me funny sometimes. And I just smile.

But see, it is all about doing what you are afraid of, within your comfort zone of course. While I decided to get a tattoo on my forearm that can be seen 99.99% of the time, doing what you fear the most could be something as simple as looking someone in the eye, or just going somewhere new and not having a panic attack.

We all have our fears, and we all have our struggles. Individual accomplishments are just that…they are for you to bask in individually on your own journey of expanding beyond your comfort zone.

Getting a tattoo on my forearm was scary for me. Not shaving my legs and going without a bra for an unknown amount of time was scary for me.

Acknowledge your fears. Be real and honest with yourself about what you feel you can and can't accomplish and just try something scary. You'd be surprised at the outcome, no matter what it is.

The Self-Care Approach:

I had to learn to take care of myself in a new way. I wanted to discover what it truly meant to take care of myself. I needed a mental makeover to take me from physical appearances over health and happiness to actual physical health and happiness.

It wasn't just the fuzzy legs that prevented me from seeing I was beautiful. Over the course of two years I have found that I don't need to wear a bra every day to feel good about myself, although my Mom would say differently (you'll see what I mean in a few chapters).

Why am I considered a dirty hippy, or dare I say a feminist of the bra-burning type, for making a simple choice not to wear a bra for my own personal health and happiness? (And no, I didn't burn my bras by the way. I still have one after donating the rest. It just sits at the back of my sock and underwear drawer for the day I feel I need it).

Ultimately, this little experiment forced me out of my comfort zone. Or rather, my tiny little comfort box. The bra was really just a shield for my insecurities. The long pants were just a cover up for my perceived flaws. The baggy clothes covered up my density perception issues (i.e. weight issues).

The shaving of the legs was always about trying to fit in and be accepted by others. Who doesn't have these problems? All the self-hatred and shame for something that was out of my control, the personal judgments of others, just ended up hurting myself when I didn't allow myself to blossom as I needed to.

So, I took a huge leap off the normal train and piled all these experiences on top of one another to craft one heck of a two-year ride. And I am ready to share that ride with you now!

The Start of Something New

Day One, aka "The Decision":

One could say that I started off easy. I didn't wear a bra the entire first day and yet I didn't have to go anywhere. I just silently freaked out about what this all was going to mean for an unknown amount of time. I didn't plan on a year, let alone two, and I guess I didn't want to really think about giving up the bra and not shaving my legs for good... and for good could have been a really long time.

So I decided to stop shaving. Okay, I just did it the other day so my legs were still looking good in my mind. My armpits hurt from the rash I developed from the all-natural deodorant so I was glad to not use that in the moment.

And I was home all day by myself, so why not put on sweatpants. I just had to walk the dog a few times throughout the day and people were at work for the most part.

Like I said in the introduction, I had decided to get a tattoo on my right forearm just a month before. Looking back on it now, after a couple years, I believe the tattoo was my catalyst for change. I finally *did* something outside my comfort zone. Ten years of

25

saying you want to do something and not doing it out of fear kind of weighs on you, so when you actually do that thing all the weight melts away and you're in this kind of accomplishment high.

Perhaps I wanted to keep that high going and put it to good use by learning to love myself, like really love myself. I had never been happy with my physical appearance before, at least not completely.

All the studies I've read, all the research I had been doing into my own life and spirituality and how to live a better life for me, ultimately led me to do this experiment. I had no time frame but I really wanted to go back to doing things that I had always done them as soon as possible.

It's kind of funny looking back on it but then again, we all do this. I still do this. The known is safe. The known is easy. Jumping is scary and yet it often creates the best experience of your life.

What I learned after One Week:

So, what did I learn this first week? I learned that understanding comes afterwards. Let that sink in over time. What I mean by this is that we don't usually understand what is happening while it is happening.

In each and every moment we have an experience. After this experience we can think back on it and figure out the details. A week is full of past moments...what I did, what I didn't do, and who did what, etc. etc. The *why* comes after.

Slowly but surely, when I chose to pay attention to myself and my surroundings, I was able to delve deeper into my own thought processes as to why I did the things I did and why I continue to do certain things, even when I am trying not to anymore (like care what people think about me and how I look).

You can say "I don't care" all you want, but if you don't feel it then it isn't your truth. The amount of behavioral patterns and automatic programming that make up our daily expressions and experiences is astounding. I was hoping a week of discomfort and silently freaking out would do the trick, but no, I needed a lot more time to sort through my thoughts, feelings, and beliefs to find the answer.

I started to create little cardboard signs with reminders and placed them all around the house. I put "I Love You" in big letters on a piece of white cardboard and hung it up with red string on the fireplace mantel.

I ripped the flaps off a large brown box and wrote "Remember" on one, "You are Beautiful" on another and "You are Perfect." With the last flap I wrote another "I Love You" to place in another room of the house.

Logically, I knew I was beautiful and that I was loved. But I didn't believe it then. I wanted my thoughts to start changing somehow and I figured trying daily affirmations and writing reminders to myself wouldn't hurt.

Month One Ponderings:

Where are you changing yourself for others? I had to ask myself that question because I never thought to ask that kind of thing before. And if you really think about it, we all change ourselves from situation to situation, depending on how we feel, who we are with, what we think is expected of us, etc. etc. Who is the *real* me?

First of all, you have to give yourself permission to not care what other people think of you, what they say about you, and so on. Once you realize you are like a chameleon, flowing with the whims of the crowd, you have to make a choice to stop changing yourself for the sake of other people, places, or things.

Permission is the key here. I never thought I had the power to change my mind before. Someone else had to tell me I had the power to change my thoughts, and ultimately my reality. I started looking at the people around me. I was shown to teach myself through observation. Observe others without judgment.

Think about how you can change how you react to and interact with others and yourself. Honor your feelings first. We often don't give our feelings enough credit, especially discomfort and fear. All feelings are valid, and they just want to be heard.

Still, by the end of the month I had it easy for the most part. I was a stay-at-home partner allowed to focus on myself for the time being. But change happens fast sometimes, and in my case it was very fast.

My boyfriend didn't like his job and my dad needed some help at home, so we decided to pick up and move in with him in an instant. We moved from snowy, cool southern Utah in April into the hot desert of Phoenix, Arizona in May. Goodbye sweatpants and hello shorts and exposed fuzzy legs!

Little did I know my universe was putting me on the fast track of self-discovery. I figuratively jumped out of the frying pan and into the fire of life, thoughts, and emotions.

Why did I care so much about my physical appearance? Why did all of this bother me: the hairy legs, the no bra, the sweatpants, the no deodorant and, subsequently, my natural body smell?

There are many layers to the human experience. Thoughts just don't change overnight. I was quickly discovering that I had to actually do something more than say to myself I was beautiful and hope I would believe it.

We are complex beings and our minds are powerful things. We have the power to create and destroy, to empower or disempower. All of the layers will come together in the end, but let's start exploring concepts one by one on this journey of re-discovering self-love.

The Comfort Box Conundrum

"People have a hard time letting go of their suffering. Out of a fear of
the unknown, they prefer suffering that is familiar."
- Thich Nhat Hanh

Boxes are limits of the mind, most of which are self-imposed.
Although one can go outside their comfort box to discover their
true selves, the paradox of doing so is that one has to go as far
outside the box as they are comfortable with.

How far outside your comfort zone are you willing to go to realize
it doesn't matter what you look like? How far do you have to go
until you understand and believe that you are perfect and beautiful
just as you are?

There is no need to go beyond comfort into a state of misery to
discover the truth. There is no need for misery in life in general;
the mind and our egos do a good enough job of keeping our
thoughts in a place we don't like to be.

And yet, I was miserable and I had to put myself in more and
more uncomfortable situations in order to figure out what it meant
to be comfortable with myself.

So, what is your personal comfort zone? Can you redefine what you see as comfortable and uncomfortable? Slowly stretch that zone, slowly expand that box, and see where your thoughts about yourself can take you. Here is a helpful tip: there is no box! It's a universal box conundrum.

Thinking outside the box actually forces us into a different kind of box within a larger box…and so on and so forth with limitless boxes. Boxed thinking is an old paradigm.

Thinking outside the box implies that a box exists, when it actually doesn't. And yet the mind created that box, believed in that box, and set to work putting all relevant thoughts in that box. All the labels, definitions and stories we've given ourselves, all of the egoic standards of who we thought we were…all in a box. These things are not actually who we are.

We are much more and yet much simpler than all those labels. One could say that we are love, plain and simple.

But the familiar is safe. We'd rather stay the same, stay in the box, no matter how miserable we are, because stepping outside that box, into the unknown, is the scariest thing for the human mind. It takes a leap of faith to step out of a box sometimes.

What's out there? The mind goes to thoughts of self-preservation first: What if I get hurt? What if something bad happens? What if I die?

It just can't allow any of those things to come true, so it stays with what is safe, and the known is what is safe to the mind. It knows what is safe because it keeps us there. That is its job, and it does a darn good job at it too.

We each have our own boxes labeled in the way we see the world. My comfort box developed over decades of fear, shame and guilt learned and conditioned through experiences growing up and not really understanding how or why things happen. I allowed myself to build a boxed fort around my life in an attempt to shield me from the world and my true feelings.

Why do we fear love? Because we could get hurt. And no one wants to get hurt. But it is what you do with that hurt feeling that makes all the difference. Just like climbing out of the hairless-legs box that is warm, cozy, and safe into the unknown plains of furriness, exposed to the public arena, I had to figure out how to find my happy place out of my comfort zone.

Throwing the Safety Net out the Window:

Isn't that such an odd saying? At first glance it sounds like there is actually a safety net out the window for me to use as, well, a safety net. But compare it to the expression of 'throwing something out the window' as something that is unneeded or no longer in existence and that is what I really mean.

Nothing was going to save me any longer and I had to jump head-first into this experiment and ride it out until I learned what I needed to learn.

As luck would have it, the universe brought me opportunities to really test my experiment in new situations. I was content being a stay-at-home partner looking after the fur kids (two cats and a dog) and focusing on me for, perhaps, the first time in my life. And then it all changed.

We moved a thousand miles away into the tiny second bedroom of my father's home in the desert. We all have our quirks, our rules, our ways of seeing the world, and we express our fears in our own ways. My father was no different. I was thrown into a smaller world where three people lived on top of each other and we rationed water because my father was too proud to ask for money and he didn't have the money to pay for more in bills. My partner and I brought our three animals into a small home with my father and his two animals. It was an interesting situation to say the least.

So essentially I "lost" the ability to shower daily. Over the next year I took two to three showers a week and never on an actual schedule. While it was over 110 degrees outside during the summer, the air conditioning thermostat was set at 82 degrees for peak performance so we were all a little warm. I kept my physical activity to a minimum because exercising on an off-shower day would mean feeling pretty gross. It was too hot anyway for the first few months to even want to do anything.

Here I was trying to focus on me and all I was doing was worrying about the other people in my life. I didn't want to offend anybody by doing what I needed to do so I just didn't do anything. I put on some more weight.

But the silver lining was the water rationing. It ultimately helped me realize my true self. I didn't need all the water in the world or beauty products to make me comfortable. I realized all of the issues revolving around my comfort, health, and happiness existed only in the mind.

All of those things were safety nets I spun out of fear, or crutches I fashioned to keep myself from falling and to keep myself from branching out and discovering my true self.

I brought it all back down to basics, mostly not from a conscious choice but because that was the hand I was dealt at the time. What did it mean, to me, to be truly comfortable? What was needed in my life to feel comfortable?

I thought I needed a lot more, but I was slowly discovering that what I had right in front of me was all I needed to figure out who I was now and where I wanted to go next on my journey of learning to love myself.

Discovering the Power of Words

"You must be shapeless, formless, like water. When you pour water in a cup, it becomes the cup. When you pour water in a bottle, it becomes the bottle. You pour water in a teapot, it becomes the teapot. Water can drip and it can crash. Become like water my friend."

- Bruce Lee

The third month into my experiment I had a profound education into the power of words. I learned about Dr. Masaru Emoto's work on water and the affect words have on it. I was also introduced to an experiment where the words "I love you" were written on a glass jar with cooked rice in it, and "I hate you" was written on a second jar with cooked rice in it. Over time, the rice in the jar with "I hate you" started to decay into black goo, while the rice in the jar with "I love you" continued to look fresh and remain formed. The experiment went on for several months and the differences between the two jars were astounding.

A Theory on Water:

I invite you to learn more about Dr. Masaru Emoto and his research regarding water and the affects a particular word or piece of music has on water. Feel free to search the internet for his findings and actually look at the photographs he has taken to see the difference for yourself between telling someone you love them, versus telling someone you hate them. These two little words have very different outcomes in terms of how they affect water crystals, and ultimately a human being.

Dr. Masaru Emoto was born in Yokohama in July 1943. In October of 1992 he received certification from the Open International University as a Doctor of Alternative Medicine. He undertook an extensive research project into the various sources of water around the planet.

He photographed water samples at a microscopic level. He discovered that in crystal form, water showed us its true nature. He went from studying water in its natural form, in various lakes and oceans around the world, to studying samples of water that had been blessed intentionally by groups of people or water that had been exposed to certain words or particular photographs.

He exposed water to different words, phrases, music and even photographs of different objects, then froze the water sample and photographed the ice crystals that formed. Dr. Emoto's experiments showed that beautiful words and music formed beautiful ice crystals and that negative or mean-spirited words produced malformed or misshapen crystals.

Water crystals formed differently to phrases such as "I love you, thank you, and peace" and from phrases such as "I hate you, you disgust me, and evil." Beautiful ice crystals even formed to photographs of elephants and dolphins.

But what is most fascinating are the photographs of the before and after water had been blessed with love. At first no crystals formed and the water looked similar to those samples who had received negative energy. But after a blessing of love, perfect ice crystals formed similar to that of water exposed to various positive energies.

So, what is the significance of this study? The adult human body is made of approximately 70% water and infant bodies are composed of about 90% water. Every human being can be hurt on an emotional level, and as the water can be changed, that human being can change for better or worse physically by the words we hear and take into our being.

Our very cells can become exposed to love and beauty when we surround ourselves with positive words, thoughts, intentions, and ultimately the energy of pure self-love.

What are the words you tell yourself every day? What are the words you use with others in your life?

Words have power, and once we understand that we have the power to change our words, our world naturally changes for us in response, as everything living thing on this planet is composed of water to some degree.

The Power of the Mind:

So if words were affecting water and objects on a microscopic level, then what were the words I was using every day doing to my own body, mind, and soul? I was so concerned with other people's thoughts that I didn't realize I was really taking in a series of negative words about my own self. They probably weren't even thinking about what I thought they were thinking.

Actually, that's it, isn't it? I was assuming what others thought of me but really those were just my own thoughts about myself. I was so worried about looking like an ugly freak to other people and yet I was the one who thought I was an ugly freak.

Thoughts are our own. When you have a thought, only you can hear it. No one else hears it, until you share it with them of course. Listen to the words you tell yourself. Listen to the thoughts you have. Our human imagination likes to run rampant and wild of its own free will, spinning glorious and grand stories.

You can allow your thoughts to bully, demean, and lower your self-worth, or you can choose to align your thoughts and words with love, respect, beauty, and worthiness. If you don't like the thoughts you are having about yourself, then change them. You are allowed to do so.

You can change how you see yourself in any moment. It takes practice, yes. But you can change from feeling ugly, worthless and unwanted, to feeling loved, appreciated and beautiful.
The human mind is a powerful thing. It can believe anything it wants. And the beauty of it is that it can be re-trained. The mind isn't set in stone. It changes its beliefs all the time based on

external stimuli and new information. We are constantly learning, constantly gathering information from our surroundings. Most of the time, we form new thoughts and beliefs unconsciously, or are conditioned over time to believe a certain way.

Why do you believe the things you do? Often people don't realize or recognize that they believe a certain way that is not in alignment with what they would actually like to believe.

Now, it is a challenge to change your thoughts and believe in a new reality that you haven't seen yet, or can't see yet. But I didn't say it was impossible. Everything is possible, including changing your mind.

Beliefs are not really who you are. Beliefs can possess you. But beliefs are hackable. They can be replaced with more powerful beliefs of love, compassion, understanding, and acceptance. Opening yourself up to something you can't see yet is scary, believe me I know. And yes, it takes time to change a belief, but not as much time as you would expect. As long as you want to change, you can change. Wanting is the key.

Did I want to change my thoughts and beliefs? Sure. Did I want to put in the effort to do so? Honestly, no, not at first. Did I have some doubts that my efforts would be in vain? Of course! I still have doubts that creep in from time to time.

After two years I can see a physical difference after incorporating changes into my life. But when you are in the thick of it, all you can see is the constant over-grown brush of the forest you are trying to find your way out of. Or maybe you're in a lush corn field and can't see the path through to the other side of the field.

The muck is always thickest when you first walk through it. But it gets easier and easier the closer you get to clearer waters. I had to keep telling myself that things would change. I just had to stick to the path with this experiment and keep walking where my journey was taking me.

Reprogramming Your Mind with Words:

So yes, the mind is a powerful thing. And honestly, it likes to keep thinking the way it has always been thinking. Remember that the known is safe.

The mind finds a happy, safe box and sticks to it. What we want to do is to get out of that box by expanding our minds to places outside that box. Expansion is the key to reprogramming your mind. Another way to look at expansion is brainstorming. All you're doing when you are expanding are thinking of all the possibilities to a particular question or problem.

Now, words are the basic unit of thought. What you believe creates your world, so we must go back to the basics and find the words that can create that different reality you would rather be in than the one you have now. You can do anything with your mind that you want, including thinking something new. The problem we run into is that we don't know all the options in order to choose something new that we would actually want. And this is where expansion comes in.

Words are just energy, energy that affects how we see ourselves and how we view our world. It is helpful to write down all the words you use on a daily basis.

What are your themes? Are you expressing love, joy, respect, beauty? Or are you expressing anger, disgust, shame, blame, guilt, fear, hate?

Go ahead, write down all the words that come to mind when you think of yourself, your body, the life you are living. Are you happy?

Write down all the words that come to mind when you think of your job, your career, your hobbies, the activities you do for fun. Are you doing what makes you happy?

Write down all the words that come to mind when you think of your family, your friends, your pets, your children. Are you saying happy, inspiring and empowering things to them or quite the opposite?

Only you can change your beliefs, your thoughts, and it starts by changing your words. Once you know what the words you are currently using, you can start to make new choices in new directions or choose to stay the same if your life is working for you as is.

After discovering your current theme, think about where you would like to go from here. Imagine all the possibilities. Expand. Write down everything you wish you were, or wish you could do.

What would you do for a living if money was no object? Where would you like to live, or travel to? What is your ideal relationship? Just writing down options gives your brain new material to work with.

Write down the words you wish other people would tell you, such as "I love you," "you are beautiful," "you are perfect," and so on and so forth. Write down whatever comes to mind. This will give you a starting base on your journey to self-love and self-discovery.

How to use an Expansion Grid:

I love expansion grids. They are helpful brainstorming tools when you are trying to think of, well pretty much anything. Use this to expand on your options in your career, or your love life, and all manners of experience.

So here is what you do: take a piece of paper, preferably without lines although lined paper will work as well, and draw a circle in the middle. In that circle, write down what you want to expand on. My favorite things to expand my mind on are:

"What I love doing"
"Things I like about my body"

"What I love about my life"
"What am I grateful for?"
"Things I like about my job"

Once you have something you want to expand on, start by drawing smaller circles all around the circle you drew in the middle with your main question or theme you are working on. And in each of those circles fill in an answer that fits with your theme.

If you are trying to think of all the things you are grateful for in your life, you could write down things such as: my bed, my pillow, running water, hot water, cold water to drink, my car that allows me to drive anywhere I want, the newspaper to read on a Sunday morning, the tree outside my window… brainstorm every possible thing you are grateful for and keep drawing new circles around existing circles until you have a massive grid of ideas you may not have recognized before doing this exercise.

Do this expansion grid exercise for the thoughts you wish you would have about your body. Start seeing the good things you like about your body and it will give you more good reasons over time.

If you can only think of a couple things right now, that is okay. Come back to your expansion grids after many brain-breaks and see if you can continue to think of new, positive things about yourself and your life. Over time, you will be amazed at what you can think up, and then you can see what you would like to change, what you would like more of in your life, what you would like less of, and so on. Just keep expanding. An expanded life is full of possibilities.

Here is a sample of my gratitude expansion grid. I would continue to draw layers of circles and fill them in with everything I am grateful for in my life:

Laptop, Sun shine, Cell phone, Breath, Hot Shower, Hula Hoop, Energy, Pen Paper, Cats, A Bed, Books, Online Classes, Gratitude, Internet, Support, Food to eat, Tooth paste, Movies, Coffee, Electricity, Video Games, $ in my wallet, Chap Stick, Dogs, Car

There are no limits in the universe. The point of this exercise is to realize that you have the answers; you just have to recognize them. Asking ourselves to write down what we think shows us where our gaps are, it shows us what we are missing on the surface. This gratitude grid was what I could come up with on my initial try. Since then I've expanded upon it after some quiet reflection time. What am I truly grateful for in life? The list keeps going on and on.

Practice expansion and it will become more natural to see many different answers to a question you may be asking, as well as many different perspectives on a project you are working on.

The Power of Self-Love

"We are shaped by our thoughts; we become what we think. When the mind is pure, joy follows like a shadow that never leaves."
- Buddha

People tell you to embrace who you are. Embrace your curves. Embrace your flaws. Love yourself. Well that's nice. It doesn't work so well if you hate yourself.

If you are not happy with yourself, having someone tell you to just be happy is usually more upsetting than encouraging, and it can often fall on deaf ears. Those with issues don't want their issues pointed out to them, and they don't want others to insinuate that their beliefs are wrong in some fashion, because if our beliefs are "wrong," then we must be wrong as a whole.

So the first thing to remember is that there is no right or wrong, there is just what works for us on an individual level. Self-love is about believing in one's self. Self-love is about loving ourselves unconditionally, or without conditions.

Our family, our friends, our romantic partners, everyone can tell you that you're beautiful and amazing until they are blue in the face, but if you don't believe it yourself then you'll dismiss their words as lies.

So, how do you cultivate self-love? You reclaim your power. Most people have given away their power through unconscious choices. We like to go with the flow, not rock any boats or make any waves. We want to be accepted and loved because we are social creatures.

It is not just about survival; we genuinely feel this longing to connect and be heard as we are with those around us. Standing in our power can be scary. And it usually won't look pretty to those around us who have been used to our lack of power in the past.

Standing in your power means being stronger than the thoughts of others around you, and being stronger than the thoughts in your own head. It is about reclaiming your power over yourself and self-worth.

Reclaiming Your Power:

You have to be just as important. Stand up for yourself as you stand up for others. Reclaiming your power is about noticing the words you use in everyday situations and figuring out which ones are disempowering you in that moment.

What are you allowing in your life? It is not what they do (and I mean anyone and everyone here), it is what I allow in my life that affects me. If I am basing my self-worth on the words and thoughts of another, I have given my power away to that person by allowing their words to affect me and alter my own perception of self.

We forget we have power. We forget we are powerful beings. We can change our entire reality with just a thought for crying out loud! Why is it so hard to remember this?

We've been on auto-pilot; we've been conditioned to switch off since we were children. We've agreed to the self-running programs and put ourselves on auto-pilot so we didn't have to focus on our journey too much.

We didn't want to think. We just wanted to be. And that is okay. But at some point just being isn't enough. Simply going through the motions isn't enough. We want more. We want different. We just don't know how to get there or we are too scared to make the leap.

So how do we start? We take our power back. Do one thing to reclaim that power and then do one more small thing, and one more and so on and so forth until you've switched off the "just being" auto-pilot program and switched on the "power creation mode" auto-pilot program.

The easiest place to start is to say these things to yourself:

I am good enough

I am loved

I am worthy

I deserve the best

I am perfect as I am

So, why is reclaiming your power important? Once you get a taste of your own inner power and beauty, you won't want to go back to easy. You won't want to go back to just being.

Once you realize you have given away your power, maybe even for your entire life, you might get a little angry with yourself. Anger is totally normal; it is a human emotion that just wants to be expressed. But the trick with anger is realizing that our anger is never at another, we only get angry with ourselves. Let that sink in a moment.

All anger is never at another. It comes out when we feel stupid or we get embarrassed, when we feel less than something and we know that just isn't right. And then we project our anger outwards onto other people or things as an excuse, but ultimately that anger is our own. Allow your anger to be expressed; it just wants to be heard. Say thank you and move on.

Many people dwell on anger, hold onto it for years or entire lifetimes, and never let it go. Just let it go. See anger as just another tool to show you where you are out of alignment with yourself and your power. If you're getting angry for someone not listening to you, you probably just never allowed them to hear the real you before.

It takes time to reclaim your power. Start with an exercise in self-love and, as your confidence increases, grow to love yourself in more and more ways from there.

An Exercise in Self-Love:

I learned this from a good friend and one of my spiritual leaders, Lisa Transcendence Brown. The first time I did this was about four months into my experiment and I felt pretty weird and a little silly. And I admit I got a little angry at first. Here was someone telling me that all I needed to do was love myself and my whole world would fall into place and I was like, "of course I love myself! Why the heck do I need to do this?"

We think we love ourselves, but we usually don't feel it. Had I looked inside, truly looked at my thoughts and underlying emotions, I would have noticed that I really didn't love myself and I still had many months to go to get to the point where I could feel like I did love myself.

The Hand-on-Heart Meditation:

This meditation is as simple as the name suggests. You put your hand, or hands, over your heart and you repeat to yourself, "I Am Love." Or you can do a variation of that like, "I love myself," and "I am loved." As long as it is love, you are all good!

Again, I felt pretty silly doing this at first. Like what was the point of this? Well you are connecting in to the energy of your heart. Some would call it the heart chakra, but ultimately the heart is the seat of the soul and houses pure love for us and every other being

49

on the planet. By placing your hand on your heart you are connecting to your power center, your love center, your confidence center...all the good things we use the energy of love for in our lives.

Repeat this exercise as often as you are called to. Allow the tears to flow once you've made a breakthrough into your heart center, or core being. And if you don't cry, don't worry, you didn't do it wrong. We all have different experiences. Connecting and truly allowing yourself to feel the love within you is the goal of the exercise. However it turns out is an individual experience.

Another spiritual teacher I found at this time was Matt Kahn, and he had a similar exercise for cultivating self-love. He repeats the words, "I love you," to himself in the mirror and as he connects with other people by looking into their eyes.

I like to combine these exercise and place my hand on my heart and tell myself "I love you," while looking in my bathroom mirror. Find what works for you and start the process of reclaiming your power and bringing your self-love to the surface of your very being.

Can You Get Okay with It?

This is such a fun question, isn't it? Can you get okay with it? Can I get okay with what? Well, everything! Think about anything and everything in your life, and see what you are NOT okay with in this moment. Then ask yourself if you CAN get okay with it.

This is about getting okay with the parts of your story that you can't change right now. Only you can answer this question, and only you can get okay with whatever it is that you think is bothering you or that you wish would change.

I had to find a way to get okay with a body and physical appearance that I had never really been okay with before…well since I was ten years old at least. When I was younger than that I don't recall being concerned with how I looked in the eyes of others. I was a free spirit then. I played, I expressed myself.

And then it all changed when I started allowing the thoughts and beliefs of others about my own self to affect the way I acted and how I thought. I became a very shy and introverted person. I didn't go outside to play anymore. I didn't make new friends because my old friends said all these horrible things to me. And now it was time to get okay with my past and get okay with who I was in the moment as I was working towards becoming the best version of me possible.

So, can you get okay with your appearance? How about your life? Twenty some years of body shaming wasn't going to correct itself overnight. I had to accept it was going to take time and effort to change my thoughts and habits regarding my body.

We all have our own struggles. Mine was physical appearance. I never thought I was good enough, attractive enough, worthy enough (since the age of ten or so). Not wearing a bra was hard for me to do. Not shaving was hard for me. I had to get okay with those kinds of things. I had to strip down to basics to find who I truly was and get over the outward stuff that doesn't truly matter in the end.

Getting okay with yourself is ultimately a choice. Can you get okay with things you can't change? Can you get okay with the things you can change? Different choices get different results.

Change doesn't have to be hard, just pick one thing you can do differently right here, right now, that moves you in the direction you want to go. No matter what happened in the past, can you get okay with it now so you can move on? If not, that is okay too. When you are ready, your problems will still be there for you to face.

Once you get okay with a certain person, place, thing, or event that has happened in your life, it'll be as if you've removed a link in a chain of events and all thoughts, beliefs, and stories that came after fall apart as well.

I just remembered that my family moved across the city and I transferred schools when I was seven or eight years old. My new elementary school was right across the street so I got to walk myself to class every day by myself.

I remember the first day of school, I had an idea of where to go but I was super nervous. I was all dressed up in a nice dress and my hair was down with a cute little barrette pulling my bangs back out of my face.

As soon as I got to the side of the building to walk around to where the kids lined up before the bell rung, a group of four little boys surrounded me, threw rocks at me and called me a "faggot".… apparently they didn't know what the world meant and neither did I at the time. But it was a scary experience.

I had a ton of friends at my old school, I was accepted and loved there having grown up with those kids in a smaller, private elementary school, and now I was thrown into a large-scale public school, I didn't know anybody yet from the area, and like I grew up with the kids from my old school these new kids all knew each other well. I was the new kid and I was fresh meat.

Luckily that is where the interaction with the boys ended and I scurried off to class as they laughed and re-grouped to ambush the next new kid coming around the corner.

A year later my main bully, a kid named Lester, put a dead squid in my backpack. One of those baby squids you buy at the supermarket to eat or something. And the worst part was that the teacher blamed me for it, like I did it this to myself.

And in that school there were no doors to the classrooms so the adjoining four classes could hear the teacher yelling at me in the hallway about the smell coming from my backpack. I remember a lot of laughter, especially when I had to walk down the hall by those classes to throw my backpack outside until the end of school.

I was so mortified that when the last bell rung I went home with nothing. It was hours later when the sun was setting that I remembered my stinky backpack was outside so I went back and grabbed it (it was still where I left it) and threw it away in the dumpster on my way back home. I told my Mom I lost it, which I got in trouble for and yelled at some more, but I was so embarrassed I never told them what really happened.

We all have experiences like this, and while I now understand I've been carrying these experiences around for like 20 years now, I can decide, in this moment, to do something about it.

Now that I realized this happened to me, and probably was one of the major events that changed how I saw the world and myself, I can choose to get okay with it or not. I can allow myself to forgive those little boys, my bullies, and to forgive myself as well. I can get okay with it and it won't impact my life like it did before.

Asking yourself if you can get okay with it works on many levels. Start with the things you see in your life right now. Then you can explore your past and see what you can get okay with what happened in your life. No matter what happens in life, can you, or can't you, get okay with it? Truly explore the answer and remember that you can always make a new choice at any time, in any moment.

Someone called you fat and ugly once; can you get okay with it? Your date canceled without a reason; can you get okay with it? Your body is a little misshapen, can you get okay with it? Yes or no.

Then, what are you going to do about it? If you can get okay with it, great, what's next? If you can't get okay with it, why not? Keep asking yourself this question, and continue asking why or why not.

With practice you will get to the point where the outside shell we call a human body and the experiences you've had don't define you are a person. You'll find inner peace as you sort through the stories you've created in your mind about life and how you think you should look, be, act, speak… the more you realize, the more power you have over your life and less control your shell and experiences will have over who you are, truly, as a person.

Can I get okay with people seeing me as someone that I'm not just because of the clothes I am wearing at the time? Yes, I've learned that comfort trumps fashion for me any day of the week.

Can I get okay with not wearing a bra out in public? Honestly, I'm still working on that one. I know who I am, or at least I am actively figuring that out more and more as I go along.

Choose what you are comfortable with first and then explore the areas in your life that you find uncomfortable. So, can you get okay with it?

Appreciation vs Gratitude

"Be content with what you have; rejoice in the way things are. When you realize there is nothing lacking, the whole world belongs to you."

- Lao Tzu

Mosquito Love:

First of all, I would like to share an experience with you. This really opened my eyes to the concepts of appreciation and gratitude. Several months after I began this experiment I was fortunate to have the opportunity to fly to the island of Kauai and experience a "sacred ascension journey" with my friend and spiritual teacher, Lisa Transcendence Brown.

Before this experience I thought all those people who spent thousands of dollars to go on retreats where they paid someone to kick their ass on all levels: physically, mentally, emotionally, and spiritually, were crazy. And yet that is exactly what I did, and I am forever grateful for that experience. But I'm getting ahead of myself!

So what do mosquitos have to do with gratitude and appreciation? They're literal blood-suckers whose actions can cause soreness, itchiness and all manners of discomfort. Well I was working through a lot of stuff on this sacred ascension journey.

I had a lot of anger one day when we decided to take a hike through a forest to find a waterfall. Sounds amazing, doesn't it? Well I had to hike barefoot through the muddy brush up and down steep inclines to do it. Now, when I said "had to" no one really forced me to do it, but my friends thought it would help connect me to the earth and ultimately myself. I was already a little grumpy that day.

And slipping and sliding down a steep incline in the mud, trying not to fall, poking my feet on plants and tree roots....I was just not having it. I was the last in line of our four-person hike team, and for good reason. I needed that space to get a LOT of anger, frustration, and irritation out of my system. I was cursing and grumbling, and I should remind you that I chose to do this AND pay someone for it too.

Well, it was a nice warm, humid day and my mosquito friends were out in force. I was in shorts and a tank top, no shoes...you get where this is going? The hike to and from the waterfall was a couple hours and in that time I was unaware of exactly how much of an all-you-can-eat mosquito buffet I was becoming.

I was a little preoccupied with grumpiness about the whole situation, which is really silly looking back on it because I was in paradise experiencing the pure beauty of nature and universal connection but in my mind I just wanted to go home and be anywhere else but there. This sacred ascension journey also taught me a lot about being present, but that's for later.

So we get back to the house after the hike and sure I was a little sweaty and itchy from the humidity and physical exercise, but as the hours went by after cleaning up and settling in, I really started to itch. I had bright red bumps everywhere from my little mosquito friends (we're totally buddies now after this whole experience, any mosquito, anywhere. We're cool now) and it would only get worse as the hours went on.

You try not to scratch but then you drive yourself crazy *thinking* about not scratching yourself. Bed time rolled around and I just couldn't sleep. I had a long day, with so many heavy emotions going on, that I just tossed and turned all night.

I even had to go out to the couch so my boyfriend could actually sleep in the bed. The mosquitos didn't even touch him, even though he was in shorts and no shoes and had an amazing time enjoying the trees and the waterfall. I was on that couch for eight hours, crying, itching, exhausted, in pain, uncomfortable to say the least.

As the sun was coming up I moved to the bench outside on the lanai and I just cried and cried. I decided to try and be grateful for that night. Many spiritual teachers I had found were all telling me the same thing, be grateful, show appreciation.

Why the hell should I be grateful for being an all-you-can-eat mosquito buffet the day before? What was the point in that? Well, I gave it a try.

I sat there on that plastic loveseat out on the lanai with the sun rising in front of me, surrounded my lush green palm and coconut trees, with the sounds of the waves crashing on the ocean nearby, and I just cried and laughed as I repeated "thank you" over and over again.

And the more I let go, the more I *felt* grateful for that experience, the itching became less and less intense and even some of the bumps were disappearing. They just literally disappeared, gone, like they didn't exist the night before.

A new mosquito friend visited me on that bench and I just watched him land on my leg and I surrendered, I got okay with him feeding on me or not, I didn't care. He didn't feed on me and I didn't form any new itchy bumps after he was gone. I got okay with it and I appreciated the entire hike experience, fully. And within a couple hours I felt amazing. I still had some bumps but a lot of them were going away, and I didn't itch. I didn't need to fight the urge to scratch anymore and I was able to take a well-deserved nap.

Within days of continued gratitude all the bumps were gone and it was as if it didn't even happen. How does something like this work? Only the universe knows for sure, but the power of gratitude and appreciation can be felt on a human level and we can use it to our advantage.

So, what did I learn from my Kauai experience? I learned that I could let go of things I couldn't control. I let go of the anger, the irritation of the day and the mosquitos. In this moment, how am I choosing to be? All that matters is this moment.

I look at my body now and what do I choose to see? I choose beauty and love now. I don't worry as much about the things I can't control, especially when it comes to my body. If my body needs some weight and extra hair on it in order for me to learn to transcend that experience, then that is what is going to happen.

I started to notice that it was more about how I felt about myself on the inside and not about what was on the outside. Logically it is easier to understand this, but until you truly experience it for yourself it is hard to embody it. Practicing gratitude and appreciation is the easy way to get to that embodiment.

We each have to find it within ourselves to be grateful for all the things that happen in our life, no matter if we think those experiences are "good" or "bad" or somewhere in between. I invite you to explore gratitude on your own as I truly believe it is one of the most healing experiences one can have.

Deepest Gratitude and Appreciation:

So what is the difference between gratitude and appreciation? I see gratitude as an expression of love for the physical things in our lives (being grateful for the sun, the trees, the clouds, bugs, shoes, etc.) and appreciation as an expression of love for experiences (mosquitos, exhaustion, traveling, lessons learned, etc.).

But essentially gratitude and appreciation are the same thing, and are often interchangeable. You can be grateful for the sun shining and you can be grateful for sun burns. You can appreciate the trees and the shade they give you on a sunny day. Use whatever one feels right to you or use both as you see fit. There is no wrong way to be grateful and appreciative for the people, places, things, and experiences you have in your life.

Gratitude and appreciation is simply focused intention. Add gratitude and appreciation to your journey of self-love on top of getting okay with what you have right now. Express gratitude and appreciation in every moment and see how your life changes. If it doesn't work for you, then go back to your old ways that do work.

But if you can give gratitude a chance for a solid month, week, day, or even just one minute you could start a chain of events where gratitude is your core essence of being. Just one minute of focused intention on being thankful for something, anything, in your life has profound effects on the body.

Remember the power of words? "Thank you" was one of the words or phrases exposed to water in Dr. Emoto's experiments and a perfect, beautiful ice crystal formed to these words. Just imagine what they can do to the water in your own body over time with more and more practice!

I can't exactly tell you how to find gratitude. You'll get to it on your own, in your own way. I can't tell you to be grateful for all your experiences, or to be grateful for the body you have, as it is right now.

Only you can decide to be grateful and actively work towards it. I've shown you the science and I've shared an amazing experience I've had. Only you can find that place where your heart sings and your soul cries in absolute joy, no matter what has happened to you.

You can choose to thank your body for what it does for you. The human body is our life vehicle, the seat of which we experience everything around us. It takes care of our breathing, digesting, pumping blood and oxygen automatically. It takes care of these things so we don't have to worry about them. If we spent our whole life remembering to breathe in and out, we wouldn't have time to experience all the other things life has to offer.

And yet we sit on the sidelines most of the time, too scared to do anything because of a thought: a thought that we are not good enough, beautiful enough, smart enough, and so on. The truth is that we are enough. You are enough. More than enough, even. Be grateful for the things you have now and your world will give you more reasons to be grateful for in return.

Even taking a shower can be a profoundly grateful experience. After six months of saying "thank you" every time I had a hot shower and a roof over my head every morning I bawled my eyes out one day as I *felt* deep appreciation.

It honestly felt funny at first, saying "thank you" for water and food, but then again there are many people in the world who do not have access to these kinds of things. I've even started being thankful for cold showers when that was the only thing available.

We have a choice in every moment to love or to hate, to appreciate or to complain. It takes time to truly feel gratitude and appreciation because, again, we have been conditioned to take things for granted and not put our love and attention on the little things in life.

All I ask is that you try a gratitude or appreciation exercise in your own life. Again, if it doesn't work for you, then no harm done, right? I am grateful for hair growth, even the growth of hair on my legs, because there are people in the world who can't grow hair at all.

I can choose to accept my fuzzy legs, my mismatched breasts, and my choices in wardrobe; because they are my experiences and only I can get okay with them.

Practice Makes Perfect

I never asked anybody what they thought about my appearance, except for my boyfriend who kept assuring me that it was never an issue. Any thought I had about shame or embarrassment being around other people was self-induced. I let my imagination run wild thinking of all the possibilities, mostly negative, of what other people could think of me.

When in reality, I was just reinforcing what I thought about myself. Why did I have a problem with my body? Where did that come from? It's not impossible to change how we think; we only think that it is too hard to do so, so we never even try. We like easy and we fear change. Well, we change all the time. We should be used to it by now!

If you don't work on yourself, who will? This is your journey. This is your mind. Those are your thoughts and beliefs. Your story is unique. Rewrite your story if you have to. Practice self-love and it will become more natural in all aspects of your life.

One has to do the work in order to change their thoughts about their reality. If you don't like how you see yourself, remember you have the power to change it, and you just have to put in the conscious effort. And I say conscious because it's not just a casual thought here and there about wanting to love yourself for who you are. It doesn't work that way, unfortunately, for the human mind. You have to remember, and keep reinforcing, the positive truth: that all we are is perfection and love, until it becomes a habit, or second-nature.

Practice makes perfect so if you haven't started telling yourself you love yourself by now after reading this far into this book, take a moment to do so. Put down the book, find a mirror, and repeat "I love myself" or "I love you" while staring into your own eyes (it helps to focus on one eye and switch back and forth after a while) in the mirror. Or if you would prefer to kick back on the couch or lie down in bed for a moment and really connect with yourself that is great too. Whatever works best for you!

I set an alarm on my phone to go off at 6am, 12pm, and 6pm with the reminder "love yourself." I also have it written on my bathroom mirror so every time I brush my teeth I remember to say out loud that I love myself.

We all forget to love ourselves, and that is okay. It is handy to have a reminder set up in advance like an alarm clock, or to place notes to yourself throughout your home, apartment, car, office area, etc. If you want to learn to love yourself, you have to practice it.

Unless you have been raised to love yourself since you were a child, most of us have had quite the opposite education and it needs to become a new habit by repeatedly telling yourself you are loved until you believe it and it becomes so natural that you don't need reminders anymore. Change is a process that can lead to transformation, if you allow yourself to do so that is.

The Power of Presence:

Keeping it present helps reinforce a new behavior, thought, program, way of life...however you want to it. Fears, doubts, and worry, among other emotions, all exist in another time, another moment, particularly the future moment. Past moments can influence our emotions as well and we often fear a certain experience repeating itself.

Why is being present so powerful? And why do we have to practice it? Again, if you haven't been raised in a household where meditation, self-reflection, open communication and unconditional love were present all the time, you need to form a new habit through conscious reinforcement.

Operating from the present moment allows you to see what is happening, well, in the present moment. Bringing your thoughts back to the "now" allows you to create change and form a new habit. And this works for any habit, thought, or belief you want to change in your life.

Presence is a skill, and we all have the capacity to master it. Our fears and doubts can run amok and create elaborate stories that happen in future times we never actually arrive in. We have allowed our human minds to create these fantasy worlds where we plan for all the "bad" things that could happen, and thus we keep ourselves in a state of stasis because change is ultimately scary as an unknown variable.

So how do you become present? Well you can't stop yourself from having a thought (that is actually highly improbable). The goal of meditation is not stop a thought but to not allow that thought to affect you.

It is impossible to stop a thought, by the way, but we can actively change our thoughts by looking at where we have given our power away to them and where we have allowed thoughts to form that we don't agree with. We have human minds, and human minds think. The trick is to train our minds to think the way we want to, and we start by getting present.

I use two tricks for bringing my thoughts back into the present moment: "that's ridiculous," and "thank you for sharing." When I notice my mind weaving an elaborate story of something that hasn't happened yet and it sounds pretty ridiculous, I just mentally say "that's ridiculous." Now, the trick with this one here is to not have any judgment or shame your mind. Do NOT call your mind crazy. That is counter-productive.

When your mind is telling tales that are so far out there that they would never actually happen, that is when you use "that's ridiculous" to tell your mind that "no, I'm not believing that anymore, that would never happen." Remember, no judgment, no shame. We are brilliant story tellers. We can think up many seemingly impossible things.

But when your mind is going on and on about what you are going to wear to Susan's party next week (like over 7 days from now next week), and that you can't wear what you want because Susan doesn't like the color blue and whatever other ridiculous reason your mind makes up, feel free to tell your mind that it is being ridiculous.

Bring it back to the present moment. The more you practice it, the less your mind actually does this kind of thing. It is like re-training your brain to think a new thought, to tell a new story, and slowly but surely you're singing a new tune.

Now, the second trick works for any story or thought that you don't want to think anymore or don't want to hear anymore. "Thank you for sharing" acknowledges your mind and its needs to tell a good story and be heard, while simultaneously showing respect and gratitude, two powerful forces in the universe.

Even thinking about what you are going to have for dinner ten hours from now, just say "thank you for sharing, we'll get there when we get there" to bring your thoughts back to the now. Your mind tells an elaborate story of the dress you were going to wear to Susan's party and how furry it's going to get from her two cats, and that you'll probably spill wine on it because you are so clumsy…. "Thank you for sharing mind, that is an amazing story, but I'm gonna stop you right there" …and then your mind stops for a moment.

If it picks the story back up, great, "thank you for sharing." The story will get shorter and shorter as your mind tries to pull your attention back away from the present moment and starts to stick to the basic highlights of what it wants to share with you. Keep practicing, keep catching yourself when you're thinking of a moment other than this one right now, and notice when your mind brings up thoughts, beliefs, past stories, and future fears that are contradicting to your new beliefs of self-love.

Remember, the mind likes its safe box and will do everything it can to keep you there with it. When your mind starts spinning stories about how ugly, worthless and un-loveable you are, say thank you for sharing, and think a new thought.

I Have a Choice?

"Waking up to who you are requires letting go of who you imagine
yourself to be."
- Alan Watts

Everyone is responsible for their own lives and their own choices.
These choices affect how we see ourselves and the world around
us. Choice is personal. I choose to think a certain way, to say
something about myself, to love myself or to hate myself...it is all
my choice.

How I choose to react to others is a choice I make every time I
interact with another person. How I choose to react to my own
thoughts is all on me as well. No one else can decide for me. No
one else can choose how I see myself.

If I wanted to keep feeling sorry for myself, to deprecate myself
and my self-worth, to lower my expectations of myself on behalf
of others, or to hate myself and my body, then that is my choice.
But now I know I have that choice and I am able to make a new
one in any moment that I feel suits me better.

Learning how to choose in your own best interest is a skill best
practiced over time. I never really looked at who I was before, or

who I wanted to become. I was too focused on being someone I thought everyone else wanted to see in me. Who was I? Why did having fuzzy legs make me feel like less of a person?

This entire experiment began with a choice (well a few choices to be exact). I chose to stop shaving my legs. I chose to stop wearing a bra. I chose to wear sweatpants everywhere I went in public unless it was a hot day and I exposed my fuzzy legs in shorts. I chose to take a more natural approach to my health; body, mind, and soul. I chose to find out why I didn't love myself as I was and I chose to figure out a way to do so.

Only you know what you need. Only you know what you really want out of life. And sometimes it takes a little time to figure it all out. But as long as you are making the choice to stick with it, the answers you are searching for will come.

No one can force us into a decision, we only think they do. Then we get to blame whatever happens on them or any other outside force so we don't have to take responsibility for ourselves. Loving yourself is a personal responsibility. What is right? What is wrong? Do you feel others are treating you the way you should be treated? The way you want to be treated? If you want others to love you for who you are, it helps to start by loving yourself for who you are.

Everything becomes a conscious choice in the moment. You always have a choice. "From this moment forward..." the past doesn't exist anymore. You get to make a new choice, and this is what I chose to do in April 2014 and continued having to make that choice over and over again over the years. If the choice feels right for you, then go for it.

If you start to feel uneasy about it, re-adjust your choices and continue along the path. Whatever someone says, or does in the moment, see how you feel and adjust your own course. We all have the power to do this, through our choices. We get to make a new choice and we can get to the point where all we do is live in love, magic, and bliss in every moment.

Choose to love yourself, or not. Choose to change, or remain the same. Choose to love others as they deserve to be loved, even if they don't love themselves yet.

Some people think wearing comfy sweatpants out in public means that person has no respect for themselves, and yet that person could be feeling really crappy or have a million things going on. I chose to wear certain clothes as a conscious decision to see my reactions and the reactions of others around me.

I ultimately chose not to shower every day because I wanted to save on water, I realized that I didn't need to shower every day at the time, and I discovered that whether I showered or not, it had no basis on who I was as a person.

So, why do you do the things you do? Only you can answer that. We choose our actions and reactions in every moment.

Why did I hate my body? I chose to at the time. I don't think it was entirely conscious at first. I took in so much information as a child from many sources: television, advertisements, the kids at school, and my own family to name a few. But now I am more conscious of my thoughts and actions towards myself and I can make a new choice about how I see myself at any time.

My life has continued to snowball from the moment I choose to actively confront my fears and work on my own thoughts. Choose amazing if you can, I know I try to whenever I can.

The Cheesecake Conundrum

"Some people feel the rain. Others just get wet."
- Bob Marley

Nine months into my experiment, everything I have learned so far was tested in ways I didn't even think were possible before. After nine months I was feeling better about myself. I had gotten over a lot of my stuff. I was less anxious about going outside with sweatpants or shorts with fuzzy legs and not wearing a bra in public.

It was now winter time in the desert so it was cool but not cold. My mother was visiting from out of town and the two of us decided to go to a movie and have lunch as a bit of mother-daughter time.

Now, I get my no-sweatpants mentality from my mother so I actually wore a nice pair of jeans on this little excursion. And because it was on the cooler side I was wearing a jacket over my basic t-shirt and no bra. I did comb my hair nice and pulled it back to look as presentable as I could without going back into my old ways.

She picked me up in her car and drove us to the movie. We had a good time and we both liked the movie. Then she drove us over to the Cheesecake Factory for lunch. She wanted to introduce me to Thai lettuce wraps (which are the only thing I eat now there by the way…anyway…).

And so we were settling in and I took off my jacket and not even three seconds later she bursts out saying at a really high volume: "you're not wearing a bra!" and gave me a really surprised look.

I was so mortified. It took me a moment to realize she had even said what I think she said out loud. I looked around at all the other groups of people eating around us and laughing, having a good time. I instinctually moved my shoulders forward and inward to try and hide myself. I pulled my shirt down and let a little air in so it billowed out so my breasts weren't as defined as the moment before. I was like "yep… I stopped wearing a bra like nine months ago as an experiment" and then she was like, "why?"

I imagine I looked like a little uncomfortable turtle that had just be scolded by the hare for the rest of our lunch together, hunched over with my arms forward and head down just in case someone around us heard the outburst. It probably sounded louder in my head but in the moment I felt like it reverberated throughout the entire restaurant.

Now, I hadn't seen my mother in over a year. She had no idea I was even doing this little experiment. And the main reason she didn't know was because I didn't tell her beforehand. I love my mother completely and I know I have a lot of issues stemming from my childhood and a multitude of experiences with my family and outside influences as well.

I know my parents did the best they could, but we take things in as individuals and my own thoughts formed my beliefs based on the environment I was in. So I guess this cheesecake experience was long overdue. The food was good which took my mind mostly off the incident and she realized I was really embarrassed so she didn't mention it again. I don't recall her apologizing, but again, that is my story, my issue.

Likewise, about a week later, my dad finally realized I wasn't shaving my legs either (remember I was living with him at the time for several months now). We were sitting on the couch watching a movie together and he just looks over out of the blue and was like "wow, you have really hairy legs" and then started to compare my legs to his, which were less hairy than mine because he had, of course, never shaved his legs in the fifty years he has been on this planet.

He even had the nerve to pet my legs quickly before I was like okay, weird. But still, kind of a big punch to the confidence gut when your own father starts making fun of you for going against the social norm to try and get over your mental bullshit. This month was like having all my worst fears come true and I had to face them head-on, in person, and discover just how okay I was with everything that was going on in my life.

While I was proud of myself for having changed certain beliefs about myself and getting comfortable with myself in certain ways, I found out really quick that I had a lot of work to do still. I was making so much progress, or so I told myself, and now I felt like I was going backwards.

Every insecurity, every fear I had about what other people were thinking about me, came to light with my own parents and out in the open. These experiences didn't happen in my head. These were not elaborate "what if" fantasies I obsessed over. They actually happened and I was literally taken aback by them.

Stuck in the Mud-(pie):

It is great to have friends who support you and spiritual gurus who know what you need to hear in the moment. And if you don't have that, let me share what I've learned about feeling stuck: there is no such thing as getting stuck! Oops, did I let the cat out of the bag early on this one? Let's explore this concept.

Life is all about growth. Are you changing or are you resisting change? That is all it boils down to. If you are actively engaged in change, you cannot literally go backwards. You stay the same or you change and change means growth, change means movement.

If you are moving, you are not stuck in the metaphorical mud. You are not the same person you were yesterday, last week, six months ago, or ten years ago. Change is *the* one constant force in the universe. We resist change out of fear of what change could bring, but embracing change just means that you're recognizing your own personal growth, no matter how fast or expansive you think it is going.

My cheesecake experience was ultimately positive. I could have repeated the same story I played out throughout my childhood and retreated into my cave or, better yet, ended the experiment, shave my legs and put the bra back on, but I didn't.

I realized that I had some automatic programming that caused my reaction to my mother's surprised exclamation but I also realized that I knew what I was doing. I had the power to advance onto the next part of my journey because I knew what those aspects were that I wanted to (and needed to) work on.

When we feel stuck, it is just because, in that moment, we are allowing the thoughts and beliefs of others to run our lives. We feel stuck because we lose sight of our own worthiness, confidence, and love. No one can judge you unless you allow them to, including your own self.

What was not okay in my world? What was I avoiding in this experiment? Where was I procrastinating on my own transformation? Where was I getting in my own way?

If I felt stuck, it was because I allowed myself to feel stuck. And I had the power to pull myself out of that muck and keep going in a new direction.

Speaking of cake...:

Did you notice the food theme? I'd figure we'd take a moment and talk about food. In regards to cake, from a whole cake to a sliver of cake, I've discovered that I am allowed to eat it if I want to. Now, food is a major part of the choices we make.

Why do you eat the things you do? Is it because it's easy? Are you even hungry? Are you bored? Are you sad? Are you craving it?

Are you eating cheesecake because your mother just embarrassed you in a crowded restaurant? Yes, yes I am. But knowing why you are doing what you are doing is the first step in awareness, which brings opportunity to make an informed choice. Did I care at the time I was eating cake? No, no I did not.

If you want cake for the sake of cake then go for it (same principle applies to cookies, pies and all other manners of dessert). If you want cake because you think nobody will ever love you and you'd rather drown yourself in sugary frosting than deal with your own mental bullshit, try telling yourself that you love yourself first and *then* see how you feel about that cake.

We're not perfect. We are impulsive at times. So yeah, I had some cake to drown my sorrows. But now I know that. And over time, since this incident, I check in with myself before ordering dessert or devouring an entire pizza by myself.

We think we want one thing sometimes, but we really need something else. Are you feeding (literally and metaphorically) an emotion with that choice? Or is it something you truly need and want to experience in the moment just because? Is it going to bring you joy, promote self-love and happiness or not?

Only you can figure out why you do the things you do and you are the only one who can make choices that are in alignment with your own goals and personal happiness. We give cake a bad rap with all the sugar and whatnot, but really, if we're eating cake for the "right" reason then it doesn't really matter. Can you get okay with eating that dessert? Why or why not?

My Own Worst Bully

Body shaming is an acquired skill. Children are born naturally loving themselves. They wouldn't know the difference between a perfect body and an imperfect one if no one ever showed them the duality of everything.

Our first encounter with body shaming or self-doubt comes from an outside influence, whether that is an individual person or a source like the media or entertainment industry. After that initial encounter we start to see more and more of it and start to incorporate more of those ideas as our own because we all want to fit in, or at least try and feel like we do.

And this first encounter doesn't have to be so obvious like telling a child they are fat and worthless. Often it is the subtle opinions of others like you are wearing the wrong color shoes or you don't have the right backpack or hat when you show up to school.

Almost one year into this experiment and I finally realized that I was my own worst bully. I could probably count ten things the bully that followed me around school said or did to me, but none of those things compare to what I have said about myself or done to myself that has shattered my own self confidence and respect.

Sure, I had a few bullies throughout my entire education. I just continued their work on my own after school. And if I am my own worst bully, certainly I can stop treating myself that way, right?

It is my choice to continue allowing my negative thoughts about myself to permeate my reality, my existence. And it is my choice to love myself instead. Someone else can call me a hairy Sasquatch or a dirty hippie for not shaving my legs, but I've already thought of those things, and more, to call myself on my own.

I have allowed my thoughts regarding my body to be negative and unsupportive. Every time I looked at someone younger than me, or skinnier than me, or prettier than me…all I was doing was judging myself and reinforcing the negative thought patterns. Realizing that I was my own worst bully was life-altering.

Awareness leads to more choices, and now I choose to love myself exactly as I am. I am the only one who can change how I think. I am the only one who can truly love me in every way possible.

Forgive Yourself:

There is no such thing as "fixing" something. Nothing needs to be "fixed" when it comes to our appearances and our thoughts. Fixing implies something is broken. Fixing implies something is wrong. Our bodies are exactly as they need to be. If you think something is wrong about your body then that is the only thing you need to be working on; the thought.

There is no right or wrong way to be human. If there was only one way to be, we would all look the same. The human experience is ripe with uniqueness, individuality, and infinite expressions of self. The human mind puts the body into a box of imperfection because there are too many definitions and expectations of perfection that it can't handle sorting through them all. The truth is: everything is perfect. You are perfect, because you are unique.

Forgive yourself first, and then forgive anyone and everyone who you perceived did something wrong to you. Forgiving yourself first allows you to take responsibility for your actions and inactions in regards to your own life, your thoughts, and your treatment of yourself and others.

We give ourselves such a hard time and usually all the time. Why? Why do we lower our self-worth? Why do we not value ourselves? Why are we so concerned with the physical?

Sure, we may have been conditioned to think and behave this way. Maybe no one ever taught us how to love ourselves because they didn't know how to either.

So, my breasts are two different sizes? Who cares? Apparently I do. Does that impede my ability to function? No. Does that change who I am as a person (my likes, my dislikes, my passions, my joy)? No. What about my hairy legs, do they affect my ability to walk and participate in day-to-day activities? Well maybe I'm a little less wind resistant now, but ultimately no. And contrary to popular belief, my legs still get cold with hair on them. So it is not like I'm keeping the fuzz to stay warm in the winter time.

And if I am not particularly active one day, with minimal sweat, why do I need to feel like I should be putting on deodorant and drowning myself in perfume to cover up a smell that doesn't actually exist? The human body sweats. It is a good thing. Accept it. Get okay with it.

Forgiving yourself and others is a choice. You don't have to forgive, but can you forgive. We are all our own worst bullies. We live we our mind 24/7, 365 days a year. It is there and it does its job very well.

Allow your mind to keep telling you the same old story and say "thank you for sharing" and move on to a new one. Forgiveness turns the page to the next blank page in your book of life. What are you going to write on it?

Universal Truths

"What other people think of me is none of my business."
-Gary Oldman

I thought by the end of one year I would have overcome my body issues…but that was a bit of a stretch honestly. Thoughts resurface from time to time as if your mind keeps checking which story you believe in.

We're reminded of the past and the old ways of thinking in new situations. Are we going to choose what is easy or are we going to choose what is right, i.e. our personal truth?

I continue to freak out about my appearance from time to time when trying something new or I'm in a new situation to get self-conscious about in. However, I keep getting better and better at remembering exactly how awesome I am and not to worry about what other people think of me. Yes, the thoughts pop up from time to time.

How you react to those thoughts is how you redefine yourself in every moment. Slowly, but surely, we get closer and closer to the point where it doesn't matter what the little voice in your head says when you look in the mirror.

Your Personal Truth Matters Most:

What is really important to you? Do you value comfort over fashion or fashion over comfort? Either way, your truth is what is right for you. We each have our own truth. But the most important thing is to find our actual truth, and not the truth we've taken on from another person, place or thing.

Deep down, what is important to *you*? What is superficial in your life? Can you get okay with it? Why or why not? Can you get comfortable with it? Why or why not?

Ask yourself questions. Discover your truth. Pick out the nuggets of information that you really don't feel good about. If it doesn't feel good then why keep it around?

Everything begins with a choice. This experiment began with a choice, or rather a series of similar choices. 1. I stopped shaving my legs. 2. I stopped wearing a bra. 3. I went without makeup and other beauty products. 4. I wore sweatpants or shorts 99% of the time. All of these choices were ultimately about living a more natural lifestyle in order to figure out who I was at my core.

I began this experiment with the intention to love myself more. I didn't realize how much discomfort I had to put myself through in order to get to that point. I was going to end this experiment at one year, but really this kind of experiment never ends.

Even though I am sharing two-years-worth of insights, I have to keep going with this as I explore what it means to be truly me. Every new day is a new moment to practice self-love, worthiness, and beauty.

Every moment is a choice to do the best in that moment, to choose the best outcome or of the highest good. Love is the highest choice one can make. I try to choose love in every moment. At least the moments I remember to. Until it becomes natural where it is no longer I choice, I will have to continue to make choices.

I love quotes of inspiration and at the one-year mark I found this little gem from Gary Oldman: "What other people think of me is none of my business." How awesome is that? I needed to hear that after all these months of trying to not care what people thought of me. It really is none of my business.

I realized I needed to really focus on me. I was too preoccupied with doing things in an attempt to not care about things out of my control. People are going to think what they're going to think. I have thoughts about other people (my own judgments and biases), so why wouldn't they? We're humans. We think. We think *a* lot.

But I discovered a few universal truths so far during this experiment and they are pretty simple:

1. Everyone is self-conscious about something. And this usually means they are preoccupied with their own appearances.

2. Judgment of another is really just judgment of the self. Every opinion one has about something is just a judgment. When you don't like what someone looks like, or what they are wearing, where is that really coming from?

3. The Law of Attraction and Attention: if you are overly concerned with something, and it is on your mind in a fearful way, it will bring attention to itself into situations that otherwise would never have noticed it if your mind didn't draw attention to it in the first place.

   If you are concerned your hair is going to get ruined in the wind or water, chances are it will happen just because you are projecting that kind of energetic thought out into your reality. The energy one sends out becomes the energy one receives.

We can use these universal truths to our advantage. If everyone is self-conscious in some way, then their focus is never 100% on you and your supposed flaws. And since we are self-conscious, our judgments and opinions we have of other people are really just what we don't like about ourselves. And since everything in the universe is just energy, we draw to us the same energy we put out in the world.

If we're focusing on the negative, we'll only see the negatives. But if we can switch and start seeing the positives, more positive things appear to reaffirm that energy.

Even though I haven't put any beauty products on my face in over two years, my skin is clear and smooth from consciously smiling and repeatedly telling myself that I am loved. I feel better in general, even though I may not be losing weight like I would have wanted to see before. When you start feeling better about yourself mentally, the physical comes into alignment with that.

(**Remember that everything in this book is my truth. Find what resonates with you and throw out the rest of it. Just give it a try first**)

Year One Resolutions: The Next Steps

Ok, I shaved my legs today. I thought the experiment was over. I made it a whole year without shaving my legs. I made it through the winter sweatpants and the summer shorts. And so I shaved my legs and it felt really good at first….and then the funniest thing happened. I felt self-conscious about my shaved legs!

I had gotten used to the fuzz, like I had gotten used to the tattoo on my forearm, so I didn't actually see the fuzz unless I was concentrating on it. I went out to lunch on a nice spring day in the desert and I still felt like people were staring at me. I was judging myself again.

So why did I shave my legs? I thought I was over it. I wanted to celebrate an entire year sticking with something. It was an accomplishment, but mostly a physical one. I didn't realize I still had a lot to learn about this experience. I obviously wasn't over my issues with shaving my legs at this time. So I decided to keep going. I continued to ditch the bra. I packed my jeans away. I bought new sweatpants to at least change something about that.

Could I live with fuzzy legs? Obviously, I made it an entire year. Why did I think I had to shave all the hair off again in order to feel good about myself? What really makes me feel beautiful? That was the real question.

I loved having a good time laughing at silly movies or hanging out with people I loved and who loved me for who I am. So I had to stop shaving my legs again in order to find my true happy place. I wanted to see if I could get okay with it completely and so, (spoiler alert) I didn't shave my legs for another thirteen months.

So, what were my next steps going to be? Where was I being me and where was I being what somebody else thought I should be?

I looked at the advertisements that caught my attention. All the weight-loss commercials, the beauty products to cover up my flaws... I was surrounded by things trying to keep me from being truly happy with myself. I stopped watching television entirely. I still watched movies and I still had to look at advertisements while out in about throughout the day, but I made one little choice to stop doing one thing. And that was my choice. You get to make your own choices.

Writing to Share:

It wasn't until a year had gone by that I decided to write this book. When I started the experiment I didn't think I would write about it, let alone publish a book about it. I wanted to get over my issues. But by the end of a year I was thinking that perhaps my story would help other people on their journeys.

I wanted to share from my heart all the struggles, insights, and wisdom that helped me discover who I was from who I wasn't.

And thus, this book came into existence (another year later of course).

While I made the decision to share my story, I needed to figure out what my story was exactly. I resolved to make myself a priority for however long it took again to figure stuff out (which was another solid year). I somehow lost myself in not taking care of myself.

Was I in a dark place? What did I really want to change about myself after an entire year of this experiment? Where did all that time go? What had I actually accomplished? How could I truly take care of myself?

I needed more reminders. I had tucked away the cardboard cutouts with my reminders in a drawer months ago. I thought I didn't need them. I thought I was doing so well.

And yet I didn't make it a habit to love myself yet. I forgot a lot of the time and let the hamster run wild on the wheel (mind metaphor here guys). I had to stop the cycle of self-abuse (pun alert), both physically and mentally. We reinforce thoughts with actions. And while I was saying I loved myself, I wasn't acting like it.

What do you eat? What do you wear? What do you do? What do you say? What don't you do and say? And *why*? I still had a lot of soul-searching to do.

The New Experiment Parameter:

Then I had a really crazy idea: what would happen if I decided to shave all my hair off? And I'm not talking about my legs. Lots of women shave their heads and they look pretty freaking hot. So why couldn't I shave my head?

I felt like I had to up the game, the fear game that is. What else could I do to get over some serious fears regarding my body and other people's perception of it? Well shaving a head bald is perfectly normal for some people.

Here I was, about to be 29 years old, and I had never dyed my hair out of fear. I only cut it super short once in the fifth grade. We'd call it a pixie cut these days, but when I was ten years old my peers teased me for having a "boy's haircut." That pretty much ruined my hair perception. I remember, in first grade, my hair was so long it fell to my upper thighs.

Now a six-year-old isn't very tall, but that was still pretty long hair in retrospect. After this traumatic incident of getting a so-called boy's haircut I grew my hair out. It never got as long as my legs again because I got it cut at a comfortable level of shoulder-height. This allowed me to put my hair in a comfortable, safe ponytail for the next fifteen years or so.

And since I was already running this little experiment for myself, like a game to get over my fears, I pictured Demi Moore in the movie 'G.I. Jane' and Charlize Theron in the movie 'Mad Max:

Fury Road" and made the decision (insert crazy judgments here, although I think I actually lost my mind a little bit).

My 29 year old self had no idea what a guard was on an electric razor, so the first reaction I got after coming out of the bathroom after using just going all out shaving all my precious hair off was: "you didn't use a guard?" Total confidence boost right there… yeah no.

So yeah, I was initially embarrassed but then my boyfriend said it looked good and was proud of me for doing that because he knew it was a super fearful experience for me. I didn't look like Demi or Charlize because, well, I am not them. But I grew to love it. And I actually enjoyed the crazy looks I got from people.

For some reason the no hair on the head bothered me less than the hair on my legs. Since shaving my hair off I've been trying to grow it out. I've gotten a couple pixie cuts since the hair has grown back. I secretly wish I had long enough hair for a ponytail but it just stays short because I end up living in desert climates.

But wow, it takes a long time to grow hair back. Even thirteen months later as I am writing this my hair hasn't grown enough to tuck it behind my ears yet. It's going to get pretty wild and crazy because I am truly waiting to grow it out this time. I want my ponytail back! Maybe in another year I'll be there. The hair on my legs grows fast and the hair on my head grows slow. Go figure, right.

So, why do I Care?

"You have power over your mind – not outside events. Realize this, and
you will find strength."

- Marcus Aurelius

I felt like I had begun the experiment all over again. Logically I
understood that I shouldn't spend so much time caring what other
people thought of me. Logically I knew everyone was dealing
with their own stuff. And yet why did I still care? This was all
surface logic; just casual thoughts and musings on not caring.

There was very little work going on behind the scenes. I casually
dabbled in telling myself that I loved myself. I casually walked
around the grocery store in sweatpants or shorts and silently
freaked out. How was I going to get to the deep core stuff and
actually change my thoughts about myself for good?

I had to break down the social norms, or rules, I had been playing
in my head for decades. Why did having fuzzy, furry legs bother
me? Why did not wearing a bra bother me? What had I been
taught to believe about my body? Where did I first learn shame?
Pinpointing the answer was not the goal here. Realizing that our
thoughts are not our own was the goal. Do I really believe that?
Why or why not? Can I believe something new about myself? Can

I not care what people think of me? Sure, I'd love to! So now what?

I believe there are a few stages to go from caring to not really caring what people think about you. Life is a series of progressions, or progress as you move from one stage to the next:

Stage 1: The Surface Logic

You have casual thoughts and dreams of changing your life and you implement a few things to test the waters. You throw the words out there. "I don't care." Secretly, deeply, you do care. Thoughts of thoughts of thoughts of old experiences lie dormant for your mind to remind you of when you are trying new things.

I cared then, why not care now? Why won't I care tomorrow? Do you truly want to care what other people think of you? Or do you want to become aware of how you think about yourself? Which is more important to you?

Stage 2: A Deeper Understanding

You've been at this game for a while now and you slowly start to put in more and more work because you feel stuck between two worlds and you have to choose one of them. You know too much to go back and yet you don't know enough yet to get to the end goal.

Ok, so the words aren't "working". Saying "I don't care" doesn't actually mean I don't care. I have to feel it. In order to feel it I have to consciously challenge the thoughts that seem to care what strangers, family, and friends think of me, my life, and how I conduct myself in my own story.

You learn the difference between your story and their story and that our stories intertwine and untwist at different points along the chain. We can change the story at will.

Stage 3: Implementation

Truly practicing what you logically have come to understand about yourself and the natural laws of the universe. When something doesn't work you try something else. You keep experimenting until you find your truth.

You start to feel like you don't care. Thoughts still pop up but you know how to work with them now. You know where to separate their beliefs from yours. You know how to see your own judgments. So what? Who cares? You start to repeat this often. You find out that you are the only one who cares and you are the only one who can stop caring in that way.

Stage 4: Realization

You realize you can't care about what your own mind thinks either. Not every thought is productive. You can't believe everything you think. You can't tell who is talking to you all the time inside your own head.

Where are my thoughts coming from? Wow, that is ridiculous. You don't think you are beautiful, funny, charming, loveable, worthy…you just *know* you are. This is the stage where you come into your power, your true self and know you through and through.

So, What Now?

Say all you want. Repeat an affirmation or mantra until you are blue in the face. In order to change you have to feel it. You have to want it. Otherwise you are shouting into the void. The words weren't working on their own for me.

I had to do something about it this time. Logically I knew changing the words was working, and I was on the right track with all my new practices to change my habits.

When something isn't working you have to take a step back and figure out why it isn't working. Everything I have shared with you so far works, but it doesn't work if you don't actually do it. I actively practice this stuff now, after months of casually trying these things.

But the more I have done this, the more I understand about my own mind, the less I care what people think of me. I less I care what I think of me. But I do care. I am a caring person. I've just switched my focus to care about things that actually matter, like helping people and animals.

Had I practiced mindfulness up until this point over the last year? Not every day. Did I stop telling myself that I loved myself for long periods of time? Yes, yes I did.

If you don't remind yourself that you are loved and beautiful, your mind will continue thinking the way it always has and it will keep telling you everything that you are not. It goes back to its safe box of things that were always working for it before. I had to keep saying: "no, I don't believe that anymore," in order for things to actually shift in my mind. I had to start finding ways to actually feel like I was loved.

I had to feel beautiful. I had to feel worthy. And yet, I kind of just shaved all the hair off my head and the initial charm and shock of that entire situation was wearing off. What had I done, and how was I going to get okay with it.

The Variation of Experience

"The highest form of human intelligence is to observe yourself without judgment."
- Jiddu Krishnamurti

This was my journey of self-journey. I had to sort through all the cultural and societal norms, the ingrained beliefs over generations of my own family, and all the lies I had heard throughout my life. I had to find what worked for me.

Figuring out who you are beyond what society tells you to be is a process. There are advertisements all day long that say you are not beautiful enough unless you wear this or use this product to look a certain way. The standards of beauty are all over the place and are designed this way on purpose to make everyone feel like something is off about themselves so that they are always looking outside of themselves for the answer.

As if a new pair of shoes can solves all our problems; if that were true, no one would have any problems. Advertisements say that no one is perfect, and yet we are all perfect in our own way.

If humans were all supposed to look the same, we would. But we don't, so that is not the point to living a human life. I feel we are all here to learn as individuals, as well as a collective, and learn to love ourselves as we are, no matter what we are doing, saying, or believing in any moment.

Do you remember the "if you're happy and you know it" song? We learn at an early age that we are socially obligated to feign happiness in a group setting, even if we really don't feel happy.

That song never made me happy, but you clap your hands because you're supposed to. Hell, if you were truly happy then there wouldn't even be a need to clap your hands and show off about it either.

Proving your own happiness to another or rewarding happiness is not the goal of happiness. But these are the kinds of things we learn. And sorry if I ruined this song for you…there are many others out there to ruin with deeper understandings, but I'll let you do that on your own!

Speaking of understanding, remember that is comes after the fact. In the moment everything is just an experience. We experience, and then we learn from it. The human mind tries to make sense of something as it is happening but it is hard to see the bigger picture while you're in the middle of the story. This is where a little faith comes into play.

Allowing yourself to change a particular habit or mindset takes faith that your effort is going to pay off in the end. Why else would we do something if we didn't benefit from it?

We judge experiences before they even happen, or while they are happening, because we literally can't put all the pieces of the puzzle together in the moment. We need time to reflect and see what works and what doesn't work. Finding what works for us is our responsibility.

Finding What Works for You:

Finding what works for us is the only thing we can do. Finding what works for us is all that matters. What works for me isn't 100% going to work for somebody else. We are all unique, with individual needs, wants, desires, and paths to walk that shape our experiences.

Not only are we all different, but we are each different in every moment as well. We change. One moment we're Hyde, and in the next moment we're Jekyll. One moment we're sweet, and the next spicy.

Experience is the essence of life, and experiences change. Going with the flow means embracing all aspects of yourself: the good days, your bad days, and everything in between. Good and bad are just perceptions, just stories, we have created. Things can be good *and* bad at the same time too, which is fascinating.

So, are you allowing the thoughts of others to rule your life? Can you create your own thought about yourself? What would that thought be? Would it be more positive than the messages you receive around you in your life? Find what works for you. Tweak everything you've ever learned to suit your own individual needs.

We're not a one-size-fits-all model of humanity. Humanity is different, humanity is varied. And in that variation we are able to blossom as one-of-a-kind masterpieces, because we are literally the only one of us in the world right now.

You are *the* one and only, so how are you going to live your unique life? How will you express yourself in your lifetime? Be you to the fullest, fuzzy legs and all.

Judgment

"Don't be overly concerned about how you look in the eyes of others. People will pretty much see you as they will. Play your part in the cosmic drama, but never forget, that you choose the way you see yourself. Don't let others do the casting."

\- Annie Kagan

Here is a simple way to look at it: Opinion = Judgment. If you have an opinion about something, you are actually judging it. Some judgment is obvious, but most of the time it is subtle. Our subtle judgments shine a light on the underlying thoughts about ourselves and our stories we believe in.

Opinions show us where our expectations are. Being normal versus being crazy are two different perceptions of expectations, of how things "should" be.

Why am I worried about what someone else thinks of me? Because everyone has their own opinions on hairy legs, on walking around without a bra, on not wearing deodorant, on wearing sweatpants to a restaurant, on what makes a person overweight or unattractive, etc. etc. We all have our own ideas of how the world works and how we fit into that world.

I started this experiment to figure out why I cared so much and why so many things bothered me about my physical appearance. I was living my life trying to impress other people, strangers mostly. I was doing things for the sake of other people. I lost the ability to do things just for myself somewhere along the journey of life.

Some days I am really good at not worrying about other people's opinions of me. And other days I don't say what I want to say, or eat what I want to eat, because of the people I happen to be around. Just being true to ourselves is one of the hardest things we have to learn.

We want to fit in and yet we want to stand out. It can feel like we're in a constant state of finding balance. All we can do is work with our thoughts, really hear what we are saying, and then decide if we want to continue thinking that way in the next moment.

When I discovered that judgment of others was really judgment of myself, my whole life shifted. I didn't like the way I looked or felt, so everyone I saw in my reality I found something I didn't like about them. What we see in others is what we see in ourselves. When I was thinking there was something wrong with every little thing around me, I was really thinking there was something wrong with me.

What were the words I was telling myself? Did I believe I was loved? Sure, I told myself I was loved. But I've caught myself on many occasions (and still do) where I sigh or groan when I pass a mirror. It's the little things that truly show us where our beliefs are at.

We spend so much time focusing on other people, places, and things that we forget to focus on what we are actually thinking. Everything is just a projection of self. If I'm judging someone else's body walking around the grocery store, I'm really just uncomfortable with how my own body looks.

All the time spent on thoughts of something or someone else… who really cares what your friends think of you? Your parents? Your neighbors? The strangers you pass once in a lifetime? Are you neglecting your own thoughts about yourself?

What does it take to feel accepted and loved by those around you? It starts by accepting yourself, your judgments of self, and acknowledging your own thoughts and then making a decision to change or not.

There is no such thing as a cookie cutter image. No one fits into the proverbial box. That is the point. Although we are a collective group called humanity, our journeys are an individual one. Our experiences are unique. No one else can walk our path, as others walk their own paths too.

People are going to see you as they see themselves. The proof is in your own judgments about another person. Everyone does it. Everyone has an issue with their bodies or self-image in some way, shape, or form.

I realized that after this year of self-reflection I was still holding onto the past thoughts and judgments I had about myself. I learned so many things, and gained so much knowledge and insight into the nature of thoughts and how we can change the way we think and thus change our world, and yet I was still judging everything.

Maybe I just got tired of hating myself. Maybe I just got "done" with feeling like crap all the time. What was the point to this experiment? Why was I going through all this effort just to stay angry with how I looked in a mirror, or eating something horrible to make myself feel better in a moment, or not truly appreciating what I had right in front of me? What really matters?

What I think of myself is what matters. I was doing everything I thought I should be doing to look better in the eyes of another, but I really just needed to work on me. And I mean truly work on me, my judgments, and my opinions of myself. Where did all these opinions come from? Were they even mine to begin with, or did I pick up these opinions from other people?

Expectations and Attachment:

You don't always see the finished product when a piece of art is in progress. And until it is completed, it may look quite messy or disjointed in some fashion. Perceived reality (or actual reality) never lives up to our expected reality.

We expect the coffee shop on the way to work to have our favorite blueberry muffins available and when we get there they don't have one on the day you really needed one. We expect the guy (or girl) we meet online to be just as confident, funny, and attractive as they seem but in reality you get a normal human being who is nervous and shy and wore an outfit you don't like because they're nervous and you have judgments.

Comparing actual reality to expected reality creates an emotional response. When the two match up, the emotion is often positive (unless you were dreading something negative happening, which happened, but still this is "positive" in the sense that what you thought would happen actually happened). And when the two don't match up, our emotions are often negative.

There are a variety of responses when our thoughts don't match up with what is actually happening right in front of us. How we react to a situation or person is entirely up to us. If we change the story in our head, or we don't allow that story to affect us, then we can see things as they are and go with the flow of life. Take a moment to truly look at your own expectations in life and see where things are not matching up for you.

Likewise, we get attached to certain outcomes. So your favorite coffee shop didn't have that blueberry muffin, well you went down to the street to the next coffee place and they didn't have blueberry muffins available either, so you continue to go from coffee shop to coffee shop looking for this blueberry muffin and you get really sad because life has taken all the blueberry muffins away from you for some reason on this day.

And no, I am not eating a blueberry muffin while writing this chapter. I just like saying blueberry muffin. I hope this didn't make you hungry.

But seriously, we get attached to outcomes based on our expectations. We expect to have a parking space at the mall, we expect our spouse to have dinner ready when we get home, we expect our cats to poop in the litter box… and when these things don't happen, we get upset, because the outcome we expect didn't happen.

Human beings like routine. Routine is easy. Routine is safe. We get attached to things happening one way and when they happen another way it creates discord in our lives. We get attached to believing in a particular future and believing in *the* one thing that will make us happy, successful, or loved, and when that future never happens emotions are created and we weave elaborate stories of how much life sucks and how worthless we are.

There is expecting something to happen, and then there is getting disappointed or upset when things don't happen the way you expected it to. My life certainly turned out different than I expected it to. The trick is to not get stuck in the details.

We do this all the time though: "I'm not going to write a novel because it will never make a billion dollar," or "I'm not going to paint because not everyone will like it." We place conditions on the way our lives should be, and when these conditions are not met we feel like we failed in life.

Are you expecting to achieve a certain outcome in a certain way (attachment)? Or are you allowing all the possibilities to happen around you? I wanted to allow more possibilities. I wanted to expand. Because things were not working like I planned them to.

Becoming aware of your own expectations, attachments, and judgments will shed light on everything that is happening around you. Our minds are meaning-making machines. We need to see the reason in everything, and we can create our own meanings if we need to. But what is *actually* happening around us?

We have to take a step back and go inward to find the answers. What meaning has been put into this situation? What judgments do I have right now? What am I expecting to happen? What would I like to have happen? And can I get okay with something else happening right now?

Definitions of Self

"The world is what you believe it to be, and it changes as you change."
- Byron Katie

How do we define ourselves? What sets us apart from everybody else? What makes us the same? Definitions of self change over time as we accumulate new information and alter our perceptions each and every moment.

And yet, are we limiting ourselves by defining ourselves? Are we limiting the way we see ourselves and each other by putting everyone into categories? By putting everything into boxes? How do you define yourself? How do other people see you? Who are we and who do we want to become?

We are often happier when we are undefined. When we are just allowed to be who we are, we're happy. Definitions put us into boxes of prescribed notions of how we should act, who we should be, and how we should think and feel. Integrity is defined as being honest or being whole, depending on how you use it.

Are you being who you say you are, truly? No matter how you define yourself, are you true to yourself? Or are you constantly changing yourself depending on the company around you or the situation you are in? Are you a chameleon or do you put the real you out there?

We all struggle with integrity. We all struggle with being who we are. We want to fit in and we want to be loved for who we are. We've set expectations on how we should be loved and so we've defined the love we wish to receive in a particular way in return.

Once we realize our definitions on what it means to love, what it means to be loved, and what it means to be happy, we can see what is working for us and what is not working for us. Is that the way you want to continue to live your life?

I knew I had to change certain things about the way I perceived myself. All of my definitions of self were based on what I thought other people thought and believed. I thought I had to shave my legs to be accepted (which didn't prove to be true after shaving my legs at the one-year mark and still freaking out what people thought of me).

I thought I needed to wear a bra and dress up all the time to be loved by the opposite sex (which was also proven to be false as I had a loving, supportive boyfriend for 8 years with and without a bra and whether I was wearing sweatpants or a two-hundred-dollar dress). I put all my limiting definitions of self into a box and I couldn't see outside that box, even though I was still loved for having fuzzy legs and just being open and honest with myself.

Definitions are the stories we've made up. Are they your

definitions or are they someone else's? Did you know that there was a time before the dictionary and thesaurus were created in which people spelled things the way they wanted to, and people talked the way they were brought up to talk like, and yet society still functioned?

We've put all these labels on what is the right thing to do: the right way to spell a word, the right way to dress, the right way to act in public, the right way to talk. No one fits perfectly into that box.

Who are you? And I mean the real you, behind the mask, beneath the facade of the human shell we call a body, beyond all the labels you and society have given yourself and your body? Only you can answer that. I can't tell you who you are or who you should be. Just like no one else can tell me who I am.

So What? Who Cares?

So, who are you beyond all the ideas, beliefs, and stories you have created around your body? We get to work backwards, and continue to work backwards, until we have the answer. Where did you get this idea about yourself?

It's difficult to pinpoint an exact answer, but answers will still come to mind. Maybe you remembered an ad you saw on T.V. as a kid watching cartoons, or maybe it was something your parents said. Who are you? Why do you think the way you do? Why do you do the things you do?

And yet, the answers don't really matter. Okay, so your mom told you that you were stupid and you would never amount to anything in your life. So what? Who cares?

Maybe your teacher said you should never speak in public because you have no idea what you are talking about. So what? Who cares? Maybe your ex-partner broke up with you to be with someone younger than you. So what? Who cares?

Do you care? Are you allowing yourself to be defined by someone else's thought? By someone else's opinion of themselves that they have projected upon you? Are you allowing someone else's story to be the story you tell about yourself?

We've been conditioned to care what people think. We've been conditioned to believe that there is only one right way to be and that we have to work hard to be that one thing. The human body is not "wrong." What we believe is not "wrong."

We shame ourselves more than other people shame us. We keep ourselves in a line we've defined and stick to walking that line as our entire life. Can you change your definition of self? Can you not care what other people think of you? Can you not care what happens to you? Yes, you can, but do you want to.

That person has hairy legs. So what? Who cares? That person is wearing pajamas in the store. So what? Who cares? That woman isn't wearing makeup. So what? Who cares?

You can choose to change your beliefs. You can choose to not be affected by what other people think of you, or what you think of yourself. You can say "I don't believe that anymore." You are free to believe something new, especially about yourself.

So what? Who cares? Use these questions as another tool when your mind starts to run amok thinking of all the elaborate definitions and stories you created about a person, place, or thing.

Ok, so John doesn't like me because I like turtles and he is more of a dolphin fan. So what? Who cares? Katherine won't go out with me because she wants to date someone taller. So what? Who cares? Keep asking, keep wondering, keep figuring out who you are and who you want to be, and just be that.

Don't worry about what is going on around you. You have to be okay with yourself; because that is *the* one person you are stuck with your entire life. It is your head, those are your thoughts, so choose which ones you want to believe from this moment on and get okay with the rest.

What does it mean to Be Happy?

What is happiness? According to the dictionary, happiness is literally defined as "the state of being happy"…like that is really helpful. But if you take a moment and think about it, happiness literally means something different to everyone. Being happy is achieved in different ways for everybody.

Happiness is relative, and it is subjective. What makes one person happy will be different than what makes the next person happy. It is a process to figure out your personal happiness if you haven't been happy in a while.

Do you remember a time that you were truly happy? Are you happy now? Do you even want to be happy? If so, you can do something about that.

Although I thought I was a happy person, after years of self-reflection and many epiphanies, I realized that I wasn't really happy. I was going to school getting the degree my mom wanted me to get. I was working jobs I didn't like just to pay the bills. I ignored my passions and pushed aside doing fun things because "I didn't have time" or "I didn't have the money."

So what does happiness really mean? After much consideration, I discovered my happiness came from freedom and the state of feeling free; free to do what I wanted, when I wanted to do it, without caring what people thought of me. I remember when I was a little girl, in the time before I moved and my life changed on many levels.

I remember the kids I grew up with at daycare and my first school. I was active. I played pretend. I was a circus performer with a stage name and everything ('Princess Sparkles') when I was on the jungle gym jumping off swings and swinging across the monkey bars. My best friend had her own stage name and act too and we performed in front of invisible crowds together.

That was fun. That was happy. And it was because I could just be who I wanted to be. I had no idea what judgment was. I had no idea what shame was. I was free to be me. And I needed to find that happy place again, over twenty years later.

My childhood stage name is quite funny because, as an adult, I hate glitter. I know hate is a strong word, so I will just say instead that I really, really don't like it. It is something I am working on though. I bought a pack of glitter in 48 different colors recently and I have high hopes to put it to use and get over my anti-glitter beliefs one day.

One step at a time though. I at least bought some glitter, right? Baby steps! Baby steps, coincidentally, also help with finding your happy place again.

The Smile Technique:

This technique is very simple. Once I realized that I wasn't really happy, I also realized that I wasn't smiling often enough. My face was actually giving off a constant frown vibe. The corners of my mouth had not been stretched in the upward position for quite a long time and it felt like I forgot how to smile. So, I told myself to just smile.

Happy people smile, right? And if you want your actions to be a reflection of your thoughts, and vice versa, if you can't change the thoughts right away then maybe you can change the actions right away.

So, I started to consciously smile throughout the day. I had to remember to do so, otherwise I went back to naturally not-smiling. If you are also the kind of person who hasn't smiled in a while and you try this exercise, you may feel a little deranged like I did. Like why am I smiling, I'm not happy!

It feels weird to smile when you haven't done it in a while. I felt like a crazy person. I smiled when no one was looking. I only did it at home at first. I couldn't even look at myself in the mirror while I smiled because I just didn't feel right doing it. That was how bad I felt about myself and my life. I couldn't even smile about anything and feel okay about it.

Now, over time, the smiling became more natural. It even happened on its own. I thought about tattooing the word "smile" on my left arm to remind myself but then I just trained myself to smile every time I looked at the tattoo of my cat on my right arm that I already had. Use what you have. Carry a picture around in your wallet that reminds you to smile. Hang up reminders around your bedroom or car to smile.

Practice smiling and it will naturally come to you. This is about re-training your brain. There is an actual science to smiling. The simple act of smiling, whether authentic or not, tricks your brain into thinking that you are actually happy. When the corners of our mouths turn upwards into a smile, it sends signals to our brains that there is something around us making us happy. So if you haven't practiced smiling recently, give it a try.

The Happy Habit:

Happiness is ultimately a habit, an acquired one at that. We have to continue to practice being happy until it is our natural state. If you want to be happy later, start practicing happiness right now. Do what makes you happy right now. Later you will be habitually miserable if you allow yourself to remain miserable.

Find something to be happy for, like you would find something to be grateful for. Often what we are grateful for and appreciate in our lives make us happy on some level. Look back on your lists of what you are grateful for in your life to remind yourself why you are really a happy person.

Some of us have to re-learn happiness. What makes you happy?

How do you prefer to be happy? What is your personal definition of happiness? Mine was freedom, what is yours?

Happiness opens our hearts. When your heart is open, you express love. And when you express love everyone and everything around you lives in happiness, joy, and bliss. Some people like to start off their day practicing happiness. Smile as the first thing you do after you wake up. If you are out and about and something makes you angry, get that energy out first (stomp around, bitch and moan, let your anger be heard and let it go) and then come back to happiness when you can.

Another trick about happiness, and the human experience overall, is that we don't have to be happy all the time. It is great if you are, but most of us have fluctuating moods. We're happy one moment and sad the next. That is perfectly okay.

But when you have a choice to be happy or sad, which one are you going to choose? Choose happiness and the universe will show you more ways to be happy in return.

We are creatures of habit. And we can change that habit. Why do we wait to do things? Now is the only moment we have access to. Make happiness a priority right now, not later. If you are not happy now, what makes you think you will be happy later if nothing changes?

You have to initiate the change to switch from being non-happy to being happy. I know I had to put in the effort to change. Smiling was very hard for me at first. And yes, it got easier over time, but I had to stick with it. I went long periods of time forgetting to consciously practice smiling.

It is okay to forget, but it feels amazing when we remember. Likewise, you can love your body the way it is right now. Love what you have in your life right now. If this moment is all we have access to in our life, then what are you doing right now to have the life you want?

Sanity is Subjective:

If I had to pick one gem of advice that I have received in my life to share with you, this would be it: "Embrace your Crazy." We are all unique. There is no such thing as normal or normality.

Normal is a social construct; it is made-up concept by someone who wanted to be the poster child for normal. We all have our definitions of what it means to be normal, and what it means to be crazy.

We judge our craziness. We judge our uniqueness. We appear crazy to other people because we don't fit into their box they've defined as "sanity." What is normal for you is not normal for someone else.

I believe it is healthy to question your own sanity at times. In fact, I believe it is entirely healthy to question your sanity *all* the time. When we think someone is crazy, we are actually thinking they are wrong in some way.

When we think we're doing something crazy, why do we think it is crazy? Is it not normal? By whose definition is it not normal? Happiness is subjective. Sanity is subjective. Life is subjective. Figure out your own definition of what it means to be normal and what it means to fall outside the definition of normal.

If humans were meant to have the same experience, we would all look the same, we would all act the same, and we would all think the same. But we don't, and we are not the same. So, embrace your crazy, or not. Find your happy place, or not.

Can you get okay with it? So what? Who cares? There is no one way to be happy, just like there is no one way to be normal. Find what works for you and do it that way.

Here is a quote to expand your mind on the concept of happiness:

"Sadness gives depth. Happiness gives height. Sadness gives roots. Happiness gives branches. Happiness is like a tree going into the sky, and sadness is like the roots going down into the womb of the earth. Both are needed, and the higher a tree goes, the deeper it goes, simultaneously. The bigger the tree, the bigger will be its roots. In fact, it is always in proportion. That's its balance."

- Osho

Overcoming Fear

"Not all those who wander are lost."
- J.R.R. Tolkien

There are only two forces in the world, the duality of experience: love and fear. Simply put, if you are not coming from love then you are coming from fear; and if you are not coming from fear then you are coming from love.

While the universe contains these two forces, which are polar opposites of each other, all experiences are on a sliding scale between the two. We experience fear *and* we experience love (and sometimes at the same time). This isn't about judging our experiences as good or bad, love or fear. Life is about both. And the act of overcoming fear is an experience in and of itself.

So, what are you afraid of? Our fears expose our automatic programming; the thoughts, beliefs and stories we believe at an unconscious or subconscious level. Fear exposes our auto-responses when we feel threatened in some way.

When someone cuts you off in traffic, how do you react? My first response is something along the lines of that person is an asshole. But what makes him an asshole though? Do I know that guy and do I know the reason why he cut me off? No. So then why did I care so much? Because my ego felt threatened.

All of my fears of being in an accident surfaced in that moment, and my first response was to call some random person names and get angry. See what kind of automatic responses you have when your fears are exposed.

What fears do you have about your body? Your life? What kind of situation makes you feel the most uncomfortable? Fears also pop up in the little inconveniences in life. Fears are our blocks. Is there something you need to know and you don't know it?

New situations throw us off our game. We can practice overcoming fears and overcome our thoughts in many ways, but then a new fear pops up that we never thought of before, in a different way. I shaved my legs at the one-year mark and it brought up old fears in a new way. I shaved my head and new fears and thoughts surfaced that I didn't know were in my head either.

I find that exercises in discomfort are beneficial to figuring yourself out. You don't have to actively work through your fears like I have. There are a variety of mental exercises that will get you to similar conclusions about your own self. I needed to do my journey my way. Mental exercises work for me on most things, but then there are things I need an extra little push in my life to get me to understand and overcome my own issues.

Since I began this experiment I've shaved my head (fear of judgment and rejection); I've gone to a shooting range (fear of guns, loud noises, things in/out of my control); I published a book (fear of failure, fear of success); while writing this book I dyed my hair for the first time, a 'midnight ruby' color (fear of judgment, rejection, and hair loss); I have cleaned my house while naked (judgment of self and fear of people seeing me naked); and many more little things that are accomplishments in my book of life.

If there is one exercise in discomfort I am now fond of, it is walking around naked in the comfort of your own home or room. I really didn't like my body, so why would I walk around naked? Exactly: I needed to get over it.

I needed to get okay with it. I vacuumed naked, which my boyfriend at the time really didn't mind. But the entire time I was a little concerned about what if someone saw me through the curtains of my second-story apartment. I can't see through other people's windows around me with all the screens, shades, and the angle of the place, but I was convinced someone would magically see me naked and like stare at me the entire time I was doing this little experiment. So what? Who cares?

Do things to make yourself get over your fears, within your comfort zone of course. It could be something silly like walking around your living room naked for ten seconds. Praise yourself for accomplishing any and every task you do consciously to either get over your stuff or to better understand yourself. Love yourself.

This can be hard. It was for me. I took a moment to just *be* naked. I allowed myself to be vulnerable. And I was proud of myself for it because I was thankful for the body I did have in that moment, however it may look.

Overcoming Fear:

So, how do you overcome your fears by not having to walk around naked or to shave all your hair off or to jump out of a plane with, hopefully, a parachute attached? Sometimes we have to do the things we fear the most, and sometimes we can just work through our fears from the comfort of our own mind.

Our fears could be more psychological. If you are afraid to go to the movies or out to dinner by yourself because of what people might think of you, then maybe you need to actually do that. I'm afraid of spiders but I'm not ready to go hold a tarantula yet. I'm afraid of heights and falling but I'm not prepared to go scale a mountain or something like that.

Do what is in your comfort zone. I can't bring myself to hold a spider in this moment, but I was comfortable enough to get a tattoo on my forearm where the entire world could see it. I was comfortable enough to shave all the hair off my head. I overcome my fear of failure by accomplishing something, anything, each and every day. See what thoughts and fears are triggered within you in a new situation.

Question your fears. Figure out how valid or true they are for you.

Once you know what your fears are, you can work through them by asking: "what is the worst that can happen?"

Steps for Overcoming Fear:

1. Ask: What's the worst that can happen?
2. Think: How realistic is it?
3. Get okay with that thing happening

Now, this is the one exercise you want to allow your imagination to run wild. You get to think of all the things that can happen if your fears actually came true. Use the expansion grid technique from earlier if that helps. But simply writing down all the things you can think of is a big help.

Listen to all of the thoughts that come up for you. See all the possible outcomes for when your fear comes true. Make a list. Then, when the list is done, go over it and see if you can get okay with every single thing happening as if it would happen for real. When you can get okay with everything your mind can think of, you will no longer be afraid.

Okay, I shaved all the hair on my head off. What's the worst that can happen? Maybe it will never grow back. Is this realistic? Possible. Can I get okay with it? Do I have a choice to? Not really. How about no one ever loving me ever again because I was bald; was this realistic? I had a guy who still loved me after I just shaved my head so no, it is not realistic. And even if no one else loved me for me, I could get okay with loving myself without hair.

So, how realistic are your fears? Look at your list and see what sounds ridiculous (remember, no judgment and no shaming your own thoughts). See the stories you are making up. Scratch off the things on the list that are highly unlikely to ever happen. With what you have left, it is time to get okay with those things happening.

How do you get okay? Well, that is up to you. Can you get okay with losing your job? Can you get okay being embarrassed in public? Can you get okay with losing a friend or family member? Can you get okay with your own death?

Another good question to ask is: why can't you get okay with it? What are you holding onto? None of us are getting out of this grand human experience alive. So how do you want to spend the time you have while you *are* alive? Do you want to hold onto a grudge for 90 years or do you just want to let it go? What matters to you? What are your priorities?

Get okay with it, or don't get okay with it. Both paths are perfect. Both paths ultimately lead to the same end, they just offer different experiences. How realistic are your fears? Break them down until they no longer make sense. See just how real they are.

So, what are you afraid of? What is holding you back from achieving your dreams? What is keeping you from being happy? I have found that I am my own worst source of fear. The stories I tell in my head are often filled with fear; the "what ifs," the "shoulds" and "should nots."

A friend of mine likes to say "I recognize the fear and move past it" when they have a new fear surfaces. Find what works best for you. Begin to break down your thoughts, your beliefs. Dissect the story you've created and choose whether or not you want to believe it anymore. Make a choice on whether or not you want to believe in your fears anymore.

Being Okay With You

"Not until we are lost do we begin to understand ourselves."
- Henry David Thoreau

The human body is the vehicle in which we experience our life. Just like a car, bicycle, train or any other form of transportation, the physical body allows us to get from point A (birth) to point B (death) and everywhere in between. And like a car, bus, train, etc. the human body needs maintenance in the form of love and attention to keep it operating effectively.

We put food into our bodies as fuel; we exercise our bodies to keep all the parts moving as they should. Some of us take better care of our vehicles than others. If my body is my one and only vehicle to experience everything life has to offer, then why was I not taking care of it? Why was I not loving my body properly?

I was content, I was settling, and I was just getting by. And I was getting tired of that life. I was getting tired of feeling like crap, physically and mentally. I was done. I wasn't done with life, but I was done with how my life was playing out at the time. I needed a change, and this experiment brought much needed change in my life.

The human body is just a shell, a vessel. Every vessel is unique. We can get okay with the shell we are born with, and we can get okay with how we've allowed it to develop until this point. If you don't like your body, you have the choice to do something about that.

Are you going to allow the shell to control your life, to define who you are, or are you going to take your power back and figure out how to feel your best and get comfortable with what you have?

Getting okay with a thought or an experience is one thing, but getting okay with yourself and your body is another. It is more than just getting okay, it is about feeling okay, and ultimately *being* okay. You can get okay with something but can you accept it? Think a new thought. Believe something new. Do something that makes a physical change.

Honoring Yourself:

I created a life where I gave my power away by allowing the thoughts, perceptions, beliefs, and stories of others to run my life. Where was I this whole time? I started to become more and more mindful of the things I was saying about myself. I was becoming more mindful of the feelings I had towards myself.

What did I see when I looked in a mirror? Did I have respect for myself? Not entirely. I sighed. I groaned. I even snorted once. I wasn't honoring myself or my body.

Honoring is the opposite of compromising yourself. We all have compromised ourselves and our integrity by choosing to do something we didn't believe in for the sake of others. We don't like rocking the boat. We are social creatures, and there are many things we have done, said, or even just thought that were out of alignment with who we truly are.

Everyone's favorite question: "how are you?" is often answered with something like "fine" or "okay," but do we really feel fine or okay?

Honoring yourself is being honest with you first and foremost. Where have you given your power away? What are you allowing to continue happening in your life that you don't want anymore? Do you stay in a relationship because you are afraid to be lonely, even though your needs are not being met?

It's okay if you do. I'm just asking you to think about your life.

I have always been a people-pleaser. I put the needs of others before myself. I'm the caretaker. I'm everyone's mom. And I've discovered that really pisses some people off. I wasn't allowing others to take responsibility for their own lives. I wasn't honoring my own needs.

My own self and body's priority was at the bottom of the list more often than not. It really is true that you can't do anything for other people if you have nothing left to give. Bring it back to you. What do you need right now? What do you want right now?

Listen to the little voice in your heart called intuition and see what you've been neglecting about yourself lately. Do something nice for yourself. Put yourself first once in a while.

The more you take some quality "me time," the more time you'll want to focus on you overall. And when we're alone with our thoughts, our feelings, we go to a place where we can explore what it means to be human and we figure out how we want to live our lives.

Honor yourself first and the rest will fall into place.

Reminders for Yourself

Why do we need reminders? I felt like a failure needing to remind myself to smile or to be thankful for what I had or to love myself. And yet, those reminders really helped. I had so much going on in my life that I forgot a lot of things.

Living moment to moment means you become less and less focused on the future or the past and the thoughts associated with those times. I've been on this conscious journey for over two years now, and I still need reminders. You are not a failure by using tools to mind-hack your life.

The mind is a powerful thing. It can think anything it wants, and it can believe anything it wants. So yeah, it is going to forget a new program you just downloaded once and then forgot about. It's going to write it off as a bug, a fluke. "*Oh, you want to love yourself? (says the mind) Well that contradicts years of programming and you just said it once so I'm going to delete that erroneous program and go back to what I know.*"

If you want things to change, you have to keep updating your internal coding. If you lapse, so will your mind. Our minds are more than happy to go back to the old ways of thinking, to what is considered safe and familiar.

But are you happy with that happening? You can re-train your brain, and reminders are just one of many tools to use that will make it easier on yourself.

When you start practicing with reminders and thinking of new things you want to remind yourself of, you get closer and closer to de-coding your own programming from years of conditioning.

I had to remind myself I could wear nail polish again. I got yelled at as a child for spilling nail polish all over the carpet, even though it was my little brother who did that. I had to remind myself that it was okay to be a girl, to dress up once in a while, to dance, and to play. I forgot *how* to play. I was so focused on being the right kind of adult that I forgot a lot about what it meant to be a child.

Rituals for Success:

Forming a new habit takes time. Cultural conditioning happens in such unexpected ways that we can be surprised at what comes up when we're working on ourselves.

We could be practicing self-love and making all this progress on not caring what people think about who we are or what we do in one moment, and then BAM!, a thought pops into your head that makes you feel like an epic failure or that you've somehow gone backwards.

After saying "I am worthy" for months until I started feeling it, one day out of the blue I started getting a second voice after I said I was worthy that say "we're not worthy, we're not worthy"....and I realized that I was quoting the movie 'Wayne's World.'

I hadn't thought about that movie in many years and yet here it was, trying to contradict my desire to feel worthy. And I told my mind that it was ridiculous. It took a few days for this to stop but it was quite entertaining. You know you're on the right track when stuff like this happens.

So remember, there is no such thing as getting stuck. There is no such thing as going backwards. We can't go backwards anymore. We only have growth ahead of us. Either we stop growing or we grow, but we can't UN-grow. We can't reverse the clock or the universal time table.

And failure is just a perception of the mind (i.e. a giant lie). We can only fail if we believe we do. And if you believe that everything is growth and everything ultimately leads to success, then you can never fail. Failure is just an experience. You can get okay with it, and you can move on from it.

Find a ritual, or new habit, that works for you. You can do writing exercises (like the expansion grid or writing lists of your fears, dreams, etc.). You can do practical applications (like actively working through your fears by shaving your hair off or holding a tarantula).

I also have quite the collection of inspirational quotes from various authors, artists, spiritual leaders, and whoever or whatever else calls to me. You'll find a few quotes peppered throughout this book. There have been many quotes over the years that have spoken to me, inspired me, and pushed me to keep going along my journey.

I am also a fan of mantras, or a word/series of words that you repeat as a form of meditation. You don't have to sit still and meditate for mantras to work. Some people prefer the term "positive affirmations" for the reminders they repeat to themselves. "I love myself" is a mantra and it is also an affirmation.

Repeat the words that you need to hear to yourself until you believe them. Find what works for you. Certain words will resonate with different people. So find the right combination of words that work for you.

Here are some ideas for reminders, or affirmations, to keep nearby. These worked for me, but feel free to tweak them for your own benefit. Just remember to keep your own affirmations positive. Try not to use the words "not" or "don't." It is better to say "I am intelligent" instead of "I am not stupid." Remember that words are powerful, and the most powerful word in the previous statement is "stupid." The "not" is overlooked.

Find the right word that works for you, and make sure that is uplifting and positive if you want to incorporate affirmations and mantras into your daily life.

Some of my favorite affirmations:

I love myself

I honor myself

I respect myself

I am awesome

I am worthy

I am good enough

I accept myself

I attract good things into my life

And some general reminders:

Smile

Focus on you

Breathe

Live

Be you to the fullest

You are beautiful

Thank You

I often switch up my reminders from time to time, but these are my staples. Pick a few reminders that you want to focus on. Start small and work up to longer repetitions. I have a short list memorized that I say a few times a day. Go with the flow of your own thoughts and emotions.

What do you need to hear in this moment? Tell yourself that. Don't wait for others to tell you. They can't read your mind. They don't know what you need. Only you know what you need. Re-train your brain to remember that you are loved, worthy and beautiful.

Endings are Actually Beginnings

"I think it is very healthy to spend time alone. You need to know how to be alone and not be defined by another person."
- Oscar Wilde

Where did two years go? What did I do in all that time? Everything was changing so fast. What had I learned in two years? Who was I now compared to then?

I realized we fear change because in order for something new to happen, something old has to end. We enter new chapters of our lives all the time. We make choices that open certain doors and close others.

We transition from one ending to the next beginning all the time. But we keep going. Nothing ever truly ends. It just changes form. Energy cannot be created nor destroyed; it just changes from one form to another. We are energy. Change is energy.

So a major life event happened as I was wrapping up this experiment. My partner of eight years broke up with me. I acknowledge that he had the courage to end it, but we both knew that this was the right thing to do and that the decision was ultimately mutual. It still sucks though.

Where do you begin to tear yourself apart from an eight-year relationship? Who was I on my own? My life had merged with his during the past eight years. It was our stuff I saw around me in our apartment. Where was my stuff?

Over the years I slowly got rid of more and more things from my past so what did I have to show for myself now? How do you pull yourself out of all the stuff and the feelings and the story you've been living for eight years? I realized I didn't even have my own dishes and silverware.

For eight years he told me how beautiful I was, how amazing I was, and how much he loved me. He still believed in all those things when we became friends instead of lovers. But had I been listening to him for eight years?

Not in the way it mattered. I couldn't hear and feel all the love from him 100% because I didn't believe it myself. After everything I have been through, everything that I have learned over the years, the simple truth of it all was staring me right in the face: I was the only person who could truly love me. I have to tell myself that I am loved. I have to listen.

I get to believe the thoughts I have, or not. I have the power to change in any moment because, at the end of the day, it is just me. All I have is me, myself, and I. I could choose to continue life as I had been living it for twenty-some years, or I could consciously end that cycle of my life and start a new one on my own.

Through all the tears, of mourning the loss of a relationship and who I thought I was, I found a deep sense of appreciation for everything and everyone in my life. They all showed me something I couldn't see. They all told me something I couldn't hear.

I started gathering up all the little pieces of the jigsaw that was my life and I started to put them together to form a picture. Everyone we ever meet, everything we ever do, holds a piece of that jigsaw puzzle. Some of the pieces repeat themselves, and there are more pieces than necessary to make that picture.

Which of those pieces was I going to use to complete the puzzle of my life? Which ones could I throw away? Which pieces was I missing?

This is what life is about, reclaiming your true self, one piece at a time until you realize you are whole, that you are strong, that you are enough, and that you are loved unconditionally for who you are.

For years I wasn't taking care of myself. I wasn't taking care of my own thoughts. I wasn't taking care of my own body. I wasn't taking care of my own soul. I was focused on everyone else. I was focused on everything else.

What did taking care of me look like? I had been taking care of everyone else, concerned with their thoughts and well-being over mine, that I had to turn that focus inward once and for all. I think I

The Story of Your Life

"Everything we hear is an opinion, not fact. Everything we see is a
perspective, not truth."
- Marcus Aurelius

I love the analogy that life is just a story, and not because I am a
writer or anything, but because I truly believe in this now. Life has
all aspects of a story: characters, themes, plot twists,
foreshadowing futures, flashbacks to the past, separate chapters,
and new editions written over time.

We continuously write and re-write the story of our life in every
moment. Who am I now? The trick is to become a conscious
writer of your story by taking back your power and control over
what influences you and your subconscious mind in everything
that you do.

I was more concerned about other people's stories for the longest
time that I forgot about my own story. I focused on what I saw
other people had that I didn't have. I focused on what kind of life
they were having and neglected my own. I was judging my own
story by comparing it to everyone else's story.

We each have our story, and sometimes those stories overlap, but we have control over what we write for ourselves. What makes one person happy can make another person sad. What makes one person angry can make another laugh.

What is the story you are creating for yourself? Why do you do the things you do? You can edit your story at any time, in the moment, as you are living it.

Everything I have shared with you can be used to re-write your story, re-program your mind and its thoughts, beliefs, and behaviors. Are you living the life you want? Why or why not?

If there is one thing I have learned that has truly showed me the power of self-love is that of honor and honoring yourself. I discovered I wasn't living the life I wanted, at least not entirely.

Sure I was happy. I was in love. I am still in love. I love my parents, I love my family, I love my ex-partner, I love my friends, and I love myself. But was I truly happy for me; my goals, my dreams, my aspirations. Was I happy with the lessons I was here to learn and grow from?

I allowed myself to stagnate. I allowed myself to stop growing. I never went backwards but I was afraid of going forwards. All of my leaps I have made over the years to overcome my fears, whether physically or mentally, have brought me to a place where I am more conscious of everything that I do. And the more conscious I am, the less I feel like hating myself or putting my energy towards things I don't want to do anymore.

Once you figure out the story you've been telling yourself all this time, you can choose to change it for the better. Awareness leads to conscious decisions. Make up a new story that serves you better. Make up a new story that supports you. You are making up the story of your life in every moment.

Are you a good person? Do you feel amazing? There is no right or wrong except in the story you have created in your mind. Your worthiness or lack thereof, is a story. Your confidence or lack thereof, is a story.

We are the creators of our own realities. Really ask yourself: why do you do the things you do? What is the story I am making up about myself or another person? About a situation? Are you doing something for yourself or another person? What story are you creating?

Everyone is living their own story. My way is my reality. Respect everyone's reality as being the right one for them in that moment. Everybody is right, according to their own definitions, experiences and belief systems.

Everyone is getting the experience they chose, whether conscious or not. And either way that experience is perfect for them. There is no right or wrong. In order to say my reality is right, I have to believe that everyone else's is wrong. Respect comes with understanding that everyone has their own story to play out.

Expand your views of the world by just paying attention to the stories you see happening around you. What is that person showing you? What is that experience telling you?

There is no need to impose on another person's story, their reality. Share your story with them but don't impose. Everyone is on their own journey, and we all have our paths to walk.

Changing Your Story:

Begin by noticing your patterns. We all have patterns of behavior and thought that we've learned over time. Make a list, use an expansion grid or whatever tools you feel comfortable using.

Take a moment to notice where your thoughts are out of alignment with your feelings. Depression is often our minds telling us a series of stories (that we are not enough, that we are alone) and those stories don't match up to what we feel we want.

Take your power back and choose to stop the thought train that no longer serves you. That's ridiculous. Thank you for sharing. Just remember not to come from judgment, shame, blame, guilt or anger.

Thoughts are thoughts, can you get okay with the thoughts you've had throughout your life? Can you get okay with making a new thought?

Once you know what you're working with in regards to your

148

thoughts, beliefs and the stories you've created, you can start throwing out the fluff: all the things that no longer serve your best interest. Expel the energy of your old life, your old story by getting okay and letting it go. Once we shed some light on our thoughts, beliefs, programs, and stories, we can use that light to transform those thoughts, beliefs, programs, and stories.

You have to make a choice. Take the responsibility for your life back or not, it is up to you. It isn't an easy decision. It took me two years to fully understand it and to incorporate it into my own life.

Our patterns don't have to keep repeating. Recognize your patterns, your themes, the things you keep doing over and over again. These things keep happening because they just want to be noticed. They want you to understand they are there. Once you acknowledge the loops you have been stuck in, the loops naturally unwind for you.

You can say "no, I don't want that in my world anymore." You are allowed to change your mind. You are allowed to change your story.

We are the masters of our own reality. We are in charge of what we think, what we choose to believe, and how we live our lives. All skills take time to master. And the mind is no different. We all want easy. We have a lot going on in our lives at any given moment. We want change right now.

Figure out how your mind works first, and then incorporate little hacks to change your system and your programming faster. When you know how your brain works, how you operate, you can re-write the coding and you can upgrade or optimize the system.

The mind is just an elaborate computer. It is a complex and powerful computer, but it is malleable. It evolves as we grow and evolve along our journey. We stay the same or we grow, and the brain is no different.

What story do you have about the world around you? What story do you have about how life works? Listen to all the stories you tell yourself. When you know your story you can change the tone, the theme, the list of characters, the plot...everything. We are all authors. We are all writers. Our book is our life.

So what are you choosing to say about it?

The Final Results

So, how do you love yourself?

It is a process, in case you haven't figured that out yet. Loving yourself is a choice, plain and simple. I didn't say easy. But it is simple. And it is achievable. Figure out what you truly want. Be mindful of your overall focus, especially energetically.

Are you feeding your fears or are you feeding the love within? Self-love is just unconditional love. No matter what is going on, whether you have fuzzy legs or not, and no matter what definitions you have given yourself, you can love yourself unconditionally.

You don't owe anyone an explanation. Not for what you do, not for how you think, not for who you are, not for needing something. You don't owe an explanation for how you look, what you wear, how you style your hair, the clothes you choose, what you eat, what you enjoy doing. You don't owe an explanation for what you believe in or for your view points on any topic of conversation, for the choices you make and every new choice that contradicts a previous choice.

You are allowed to change your mind. Everything else changes on its own as it is so why wouldn't you? All life is change.

I believe everyone hates their body and their mind in some fashion. Why? Because we are meant to. We are meant to realize that we are not our bodies. We are meant to realize that we are not our minds. We have to grow to love them for what they are and what they do for us. Not what we *think* they should do, or for how we *think* they should look.

We are supposed to learn love, compassion, and understanding in this lifetime. And this includes loving and understanding our own bodies, the vehicle we have to experience life in.

Your thoughts are not going away. Embrace them or change them. We are human beings having a human experience and humans have thoughts. It is our journey to figure out how to find balance in our thoughts and make choices that come from love.

The physical world is simply a response to what we have going on within us. What we say, what we do, and how we act reflect who we are and permeate out into the world around us. Study other people and how they live their stories. This is how we learn. Expand your definitions of self and find what works for you.

Throughout this experience, I have learned that discomfort tells you where you have to go next on your journey. Discomfort brings up all the thoughts, beliefs, and stories we have avoided within ourselves. Discomfort shows us what we have to work on. And it will keep coming around until we deal with it.

Therefore, discomfort is ultimately a gift. Yes, it is uncomfortable to be human at times. We have human mentalities and we can get caught up in the human condition. If you don't like something, figure out why.

What is your head saying? What is your heart saying? Are they saying the same thing? Finding self-love takes a step back, a reflection on your life from an outside viewpoint.

And remember to give yourself a pat on the back for everything you have done from time to time. Being human is an accomplishment. Look at what you've learned. Look at where you are right now. Your reality is your own. It isn't going to be typical, because it isn't meant to.

If you can get okay with being human you have life set. I'm working on this myself. Always work on yourself. You don't have to make life-altering changes to your life in every moment. Just keep the momentum going by continuing to expand, continuing to delve deeper into your own self.

I still have thoughts pop up from time to time about my weight, or what I am wearing, or how unruly my hair is on a particular day. The thoughts will be there. But they come around less and less now and I can switch my focus a lot faster. Just keep practicing.

Start by committing yourself to the things you really want out of life. Where is your energy flowing? What are you focusing on? If you focus on the negative that is all you will see. If you focus on the positive the universe conspires to give you more positive things to notice and experience in your life.

To recognize something means to know something again. We are all on journeys of remembering; remembering self-love. When we break down the word "recognize" into "re-cognize," the word literally means to "bring back into consciousness."

We're remembering we are more than our human shells, our bodies. We are remembering we are more than the thoughts we have running around our minds. In this remembering we discover our truth. In this remembering we find the love for ourselves again.

My Journey is My Own:

This journey was really about overcoming fears: fear of rejection, of judgment, of not being good enough, of failing, of succeeding, of jumping (out of the comfort box). We've played with fear for so long. We know it intimately. We live it every day.

I wanted to play a new game. I wanted to experience something new besides fear. I am choosing joy, happiness, and bliss. What are you going to choose?

I am blessed to have the life I have, imperfections and all. Sure it bothers me from time to time about my physical appearance. These are the moments I forget. But when I remember how amazing and awesome I am as a personality, beyond the shell of the human body, the worries melt away.

We want an easy fix to our problems. I know my human mind feels that way. In two years I've learned this thing we call life, and creating the one we really want, takes constant work. It doesn't have to be hard work. But it takes work. We are all capable of becoming masters of our own reality.

Fuzzy legs, bare legs, bra, no bra, sweatpants and all…does it really matter? We can play with so much more. We can get so much more joy out of life beyond these things. Can we write a new story? Can we live a new life? Yes, yes we can.

I think I finally surrendered to the idea of change, to the idea of loving myself as I am. I was walking the tight rope between letting go and staying the same for so long that I got so tired of it and just jumped. The tight rope act was fun while it lasted, but there are so many other things to experience in life. What was I not seeing in my life by focusing on a little hair or a little perception issue?

People are going to judge you no matter what. People are going to look at you funny no matter what. We are all different. We try to be the same but we just can't be. So what can you do about it?

Focus on you: love yourself, honor yourself, respect yourself, and support yourself. If you can't find love, respect, and support from those around you, then give those things to yourself. I have found what works for me. I am happy with my life. I am happy with myself. Somewhere along this journey I found what it means to love myself.

To everyone who is struggling with how they see themselves, and for those who are trying to find the beauty within themselves, keep going. You have all the answers. Don't stop until you find those answers. Trust in yourself. Take your power back from everyone and everything you've given it away to.

We each have our own experience, our own life. We have to find what is true for us. We have to get happy with what we have available. We have to love ourselves first.

Through all the changes, it is our job to honor our process, to honor our stories. Honor yourself and continually re-focus your energy on what you want each and every moment and let the rest go. Allow others the space and support to honor their journeys as well.

I would like to share one of my favorite quotes that really stuck with me over the years and continues to strike me every time I read it:

"There are hundreds of paths up the mountain, all leading to the same place; so it doesn't matter which path you take. The only person wasting time is the one who runs around the mountain telling everyone that his or her path is wrong."
- Hindu Proverb

Finding Your Truth

Do I love myself now? I believe I do. It is interesting that this experiment into love started by actively working through my fears. I was afraid of so many things happening that I never truly lived. Experience is the essence of life, and I was controlling what I experienced out of fear.

The interesting thing about fear is that simple action can conquer it. Do something, anything, that pushes you in the direction you want to go; towards the direction of love. If you want magic, bliss, unicorns, and rainbows, you have to start asking for it. You have to do something that puts you in alignment with that reality you want. After two years I finally realized I had to do something in order for something to happen.

What action will you take to get you one step closer to your goals? What is the next step? Don't worry about what is at the top of the stairs. Just take the first step and see what happens.

None of us are getting out of the human experience alive. The point of life is to die after all of our lessons have been learned. So why am I treating myself like an afterthought? Why am I so concerned what other people say about me? Why do I groan and moan about the little inconveniences in life instead of taking a moment to see the beauty in the sun rays popping out through the spaces in between a tree branch?

If anything, the journey of life is about choice; choices present themselves in every moment. Where are your priorities? Are you going to choose to love yourself right now or continue to hate yourself for something that is over and done with?

Are you going to say a kind word to someone else or are you going to spread hate and disgust? Are you going to eat that piece of cake because you enjoy it or are you going to deny yourself the simple pleasures in life because of a negative thought about your body shape?

I choose to be the best version of myself in every moment. Not the ego's definition of best where I have to be better than everybody, just my personal best. I shaved my legs at the end of two years, why? I feel like I can now because I know how to ask myself why, why am I doing this? Am I coming from fear or judgment of self? Or do I just want the experience? Does this make me happy?

If I am doing it for someone else it doesn't work for me. But if I am doing it for me, because it makes me happy and there are no judgments about it, then great, I'll do it. I have found what works for me.

I hope this book inspired you to think and question your own reality in some fashion. I hope this book inspired you to figure things out for yourself. I honor your journey.

Be authentic with yourself. I can only help you find your own power. I can share my story, and then you get to choose what fits with you and your life. You get to choose what resonates with you.

Remember that you are you for a reason. You are what makes this world go round. You are under no obligation to be something you are not. You don't have to follow someone else and do what they say, or do something the way they do it. This is your journey.

Question everything I tell you. Question everything out there. Find your truth and live it. I've offered tools for people to solve their own problems. I can't solve your problems for you, just like you can't solve my problems for me.

It took me two years to take full responsibility for myself and my life. When you do that everything falls into place. Why do you do the things you do? Where are you coming from when you make a decision? When you have a thought? When you say something to someone? Just keep asking. You know the answers.

I can't tell you what to do. Only you can decide how you are going to live your life and how you want your life to feel. I've shared what I have come to understand about life and the experiences of human thought. This is your time to shine. This is your time to make a choice.

Love yourself, or don't. But remember that everyone has their struggles, everyone has their issues. So it is always better to be kind, encouraging, or even neutral in your interactions with others, instead of mean and discouraging.

As you've seen, the mind is a powerful thing. After twenty-some years I still have issues with my thoughts and beliefs about myself. All I can say is that I am working on it and every day, in every way, I am getting better and better.

I love you. Thank you.
Go find your truth and live it to the fullest.

And Remember, Always:

You are Beautiful,
You are Loved,
You are Worthy,
Fuzzy legs and All.

About the Author

Elizabeth Crooks is a writer, author, artist, and guide who shares her knowledge of consciousness and the human experience, emphasizing the art of mindfulness and living from the heart. She holds a Bachelors of Metaphysical Sciences degree (B.Msc.) from the University of Metaphysics Sciences, and is a certified Reiki Master with years of energy work experience. When she is not sharing her knowledge through writings she spends her time reading, traveling, walking in nature, creating art, and doodling in love. She is a published author on books pertaining to metaphysical sciences and personal growth, as well as conscious coloring books for both adults and children.

For more information, please visit:
www.elizabeth-crooks.com

www.ingramcontent.com/pod-product-compliance
Lightning Source LLC
Chambersburg PA
CBHW060929040426

42445CB00011B/855